THE TONY AWARD

THE ANTOINETTE PERRY AWARD

The medallion, which is three inches in diameter, is made of silver and depicts the masks of comedy and tragedy. The lucite stand measures approximately 3¾ by 3¾ inches.

THE TONY AWARD

A Complete Listing
With A History
of
The American Theatre Wing

Edited by
ISABELLE STEVENSON

Research Consultant
Sonia Ediff

CROWN PUBLISHING, INC.
New York

Library of Congress Cataloging in Publication Data
Stevenson, Isabelle, 1915-
    The Tony Award—winners and nominations.
        1. Tony Awards. 2. American Theatre Wing.
I. Ediff, Sonia. II. Title.
PN2270.A93S8   792'.07'9   74-28337
ISBN 0-405-06485-3

Contents

Preface

Since the inception of the Antoinette Perry Awards in 1947, the selection of categories and nominations by the committee has undergone many changes. The categories have, from season to season, been redefined, added to, and subtracted from, in order to remain flexible and to accommodate the individual and particular circumstances of each season.

The governing principle and yardstick for selecting a particular play, actor, etc., has, from the very beginning, been "distinguished achievement in the theatre" rather than "best." Therefore, there have been several occasions when the committee has selected two or three winners in the same category. For example, José Ferrer and Fredric March were both winners in the category of dramatic actor in 1947. "Fiorello!" and "The Sound of Music" both received Tonys in the musical category in 1960.

Until 1955, the selection of winners was announced, but the nominees were not. Therefore, during these first years there is no listing of nominations.

Certain categories were added over the years. For example, there was no Tony Award for lighting until 1970.

Since 1956 (with the exception of 1958), the American Theatre Wing's Tony nominations have been publicly announced in each category.

An asterisk denotes the winner in each category. The order of categories is not necessarily the order in which the Tonys were presented in a particular year.

The Special Awards presented each year were given for many reasons: For example, Helen Menken's presentation to Gilbert Miller for his distinguished career as producer in the theatre; Cary Grant's tribute to Noel Coward for his contribution to the American theatre; and presentations to many others for their loyal and interested support of the theatre.

5

The Special Awards were presented to such shows as *Good Evening* and *A Thurber Carnival* for which there was no specific category but which merited recognition of their excellence.

The award was given posthumously to Helen Menken for her years of devoted service to the Wing as president and member of the board. Other special awards went to Rosamond Gilder, Vera Allen and Mrs. Martin Beck for their dedication and service.

HISTORY OF THE
AMERICAN THEATRE WING

History of the
American Theatre Wing

THE STAGE IS SET — THE CAST ASSEMBLES

If a Tony is ever given to the longest running service organization in the theatre, it should go to the American Theatre Wing. The stage was set in 1917 when seven ladies—Rachel Crothers, Louise Closser Hale, Dorothy Donnelly, Josephine Hull, Minnie Dupree, Bessie Tryee, and Louise Drew—met to talk about the possibility of forming an organization to aid war relief. At that meeting it was decided to call members of the theatre world together for another meeting two weeks later. Word got around. The Hudson Theatre was packed. There were the internationally famous together with wardrobe mistresses, stage hands, producers —people representing every segment of the family of "theatre." It took only two more weeks and the "Stage Women's War Relief" was functioning. Workrooms were immediately established for sewing—their output would eventually total 1,863,645 articles. Clothing and food collection centers were organized, a canteen for servicemen was set up on Broadway, and troops of entertainers were on their way to entertain wherever needed. Speakers were trained to sell Liberty Bonds—and they sold $10,000,000 worth of them. The "Stage Women's War Relief" was one of the most useful and active relief organizations in the world.

Even after the war their services continued. In 1920, at another mass meeting, the men formed their committee. This time, their efforts were on behalf of the civilian population still suffering from the effects of the war.

The need for relief activities diminished, but the organization continued. In 1939, Rachel Crothers was called upon to reactivate her committee. Josephine Hull and Minnie Dupree were members

9

again, together with Antoinette Perry, Vera Allen, Gertrude Lawrence, Lucile Watson, Theresa Helburn, and Edith Atwater.

Many of the theatre's most distinguished performers worked far away from the footlights. One example was the workroom committee headed by Lucile Watson. Minutes from a June 9, 1940 meeting show that Peggy Conklin, Ruth Gordon, Uta Hagen, and Vivian Vance were a few of those serving in this capacity.

During this period, the organization was renamed the American Theatre Wing War Service, and was a branch of the British War Relief Society. Gilbert Miller, chairman of the men's division, staged a benefit to aid British air raid victims in 1941, and raised $40,000.

Directly after Pearl Harbor, the Wing became an independent organization. The forty-three who comprised the executive board and committee were a "Who's Who" of the theatre. Rachel Crothers was president; Gertrude Lawrence and Helen Hayes were first and second vice-presidents; Vera Allen; third vice-president; and Josephine Hull was treasurer. Antoinette Perry served as secretary.

The Men's Executive Committee included Gilbert Miller, Brooks Atkinson, George S. Kaufman, Raymond Massey, Brock Pemberton, Billy Rose, Lee Shubert, Max Gordon, and Vinton Freedley; Co-chairwomen were Jane Cowl and Selena Royle.

The Hudson Theatre was again the scene for a mass meeting of the entertainment industry, and from this came some of the Wing's most famous activities. Perhaps the most famous were the Stage Door Canteens. There were eight in cities around the country, as well as in London and Paris. Alfred Lunt was the food expert, Katharine Cornell helped in the kitchen, Marlene Dietrich was frequently on hand at the milk bar, and Dorothy Fields did "K.P." Alan Hewitt was Co-chairman, Radie Harris, Chairman of the Entertainment Committee, brought in the talent to work at the Canteen, and Jean Dalrymple, who was Rachel Crothers' first publicity volunteer became the Chairman of the Publicity Committee. Speakers, trained by the Wing, sold bonds. With the money raised from the movie "Stage Door Canteen," the Wing was able to give $75,000 to the USO to inaugurate legitimate drama as entertainment for soldiers overseas. The first play was "The Barretts of Wimpole Street," starring Katharine Cornell. The weekly radio program, "Stage Door Canteen" was another source of income. The "Lunchtime Follies" went out to entertain factory workers. Lunch was sometimes at midnight.

As a sample of the Wing's activities—and accomplishments— in New York, during the war and the first eight months after, the Wing sent out nearly 1,500 auditorium programs, 350 legitimate plays, and over 6,700 ward units, using, in all, well over 40,000 volunteers.

At its peak there were 25 hospitals within a radius of 75 miles of New York. The Wing was sending out about 1,200 entertainers each month. During that same period, flying with the Naval Air Corps, the Wing sent units to ten Naval and Marine hospitals. In all, 97 units, including plays, using 617 people were flown for weekend hospital performances for the Navy.

The monthly aggregate during the first postwar year was still 650 people a month. Branches of the Wing in Washington, D.C., and Boston had equally impressive records.

In the spring of 1947 the Wing took another dramatic step. A specialized recreation program was begun, and the teaching of its technique to staff and volunteer workers in each of the neuro-psychiatric hospitals under the Veterans Administration was started. Teams of Wing actresses, selected for their experience and particular qualities, resigned their theatre and radio jobs for a three-and-a-half-month tour.

Vera Allen, Ben Grauer, Elaine Perry, and Russel Crouse are but a few who were active on the hospital committee.

For those families beginning to face the homecoming of wounded and the problems brought on by separation, the Wing created the Community Players. Outstanding playwrights wrote short plays dramatizing specific problems which served as catalysts for family discussion.

Katharine Cornell and Mrs. Henry N. Pratt were Co-chairwomen. Vera Allen, Mrs. Paul Raymer and Cornelia Otis Skinner served as vice-chairwomen.

At the peak of the war there were fifty-four separate Wing activities, any one of which would have ranked as a major war service.

When the war was finally over, the Wing turned its attention to the returning veteran. On September 13, 1945 a letter went to all members calling for the first meeting of the planning committee for postwar activities. The committee met the following week.

One of the plans put into motion was to have a theatre school for the returning veterans. On July 8, 1946, the American Theatre Wing Professional Training School opened its doors. The founders of the school were Vera Allen, Mary Hunter and Winston O'Keefe, who also served as the school's director. Theresa Helburn, Maurice Evans and Louis M. Simon were among those on the advisory committee. Mr. Simon succeeded Mr. O'Keefe as director.

School hours were 10 AM to midnight, and the students were from all areas of theatre, representing every theatre union. The original curriculum grew from 23 to 50 courses offered.

To name all those who taught would be to list almost every distinguished name from theatre, television, the opera and music. Leon Barzin and Joseph Rosenstock taught conducting. Alfred Lunt, Lehman Engel, Eva Le Gallienne, Sir Cedric Hardwicke, Cyril Ritchard, José Ferrer, and Maureen Stapleton taught acting. Martha Graham, Hanya Holm, José Limon, Charles Weidman, Ray Bolger, and Katharine Dunham taught dance. Kermit Bloomgarden lectured on producing and brought in fellow producers as guests. Delbert Mann and Ezra Stone headed TV workshops.

There were courses in Hebrew liturgical singing and repertoire, management problems, and one on music for actors and directors taught by Richard Rodgers and Oscar Hammerstein II.

Among Wing students, all professionals, but not yet famous, were Russell Nype, Pat Hingle, Tony Randall, William Warfield, Charlton Heston, Gordon MacRae, and James Whitmore, as well as leading singers of the Met and the New York City Opera Company who came to improve their acting.

Marge and Gower Champion, already a starring dance team, came to study music. At its peak, 1,200 were enrolled in the school, many of them studying on their GI Bill of Rights. The school continued to fulfill its obligation to veterans for well over a decade.

Today the American Theatre Wing continues its programs to further the highest standards of the theatre. It is now sixty-three years since Rachel Crothers held her first meeting, and thirty-three years since the first Tony® Awards were given. That original idea of professional service to the community and high quality of performance continues in the Wing's present activities.

The Wing is concerned with youth—with seeing that the theatre is brought to young people in as many community areas as possible. This is done via its support of "Saturday Theatre for Children" which brings quality live theatre to the school auditoriums. These public schools, in the five boroughs, are, for the most part, in low-income neighborhoods. As a Rockefeller Foundation study showed, the great majority of those who attend the theatre regularly today are those who attended the theatre regularly as children. The Wing is concerned with building the audience that will support tomorrow's theatre. It is an organization through which the theatre can give direct service to the community.

In the tradition of its hospital program during two world wars, the Wing continues to bring professional productions from Broadway and Off-Off Broadway to veteran's hospitals and institutions.

The Wing also sponsors seminars on "Working in the Theatre". These are held in the spring and fall of each year for students and professional members of the various theatrical unions. Here, they have the opportunity to listen and talk to some of America's most distinguished actors, directors, designers, press agents, producers, and playwrights. These seminars are moderated by Wing Board Members Jean Dalrymple and Henry Hewes, and are chaired by the Wing's President, Isabelle Stevenson. Tony Award winners such as: Angela Lansbury, Len Cariou, Carole Shelley, Jane Alexander, Michael Moriarty, Bob Fosse, Michael Bennett, Dore Schary, Betty Comden, Adolph Green, Joseph Papp, Alexander Cohen, Morton Gottlieb, Michael Stewart, Stephen Sondheim, Boris Aronson, Oliver Smith, and Patricia Zipprodt are just a few of those who have given freely of their time for this valuable program. The audience also participates in a question and answer period with the panelists at the end of each seminar. These programs have been videotaped by the City University of New York's television station, Channel B. This educational cable station in Manhattan broadcasts the Wing's seminars three times a week.

Private contributions, fund raising efforts, membership dues, and proceeds from the Tony Award telecasts support all of the Wing's programs.

The Wing's activities continue to expand under the direction of Mrs. John Stevenson, who has been a board member since 1957 and succeeded Helen Menken as president in 1966.

In recent years the Wing's scholarship programs have been enlarged. Recognizing the importance of and need for new playwrights, grants are made to the Eugene O'Neill Theatre Center in Waterford, Connecticut, The New Dramatists, and Playwrights Horizons. Acting fellowships and grants to developing theatre companies are given as well. The Wing was also a sponsor of F.A.C.T., the First American Congress of Theatre, held in Princeton, New Jersey in 1974.

Isabelle Stevenson, like her predecessors, had been actively engaged in the theatre and, prior to her marriage, appeared in theatres throughout the country, Europe and Australia. She is active in theatre and community-oriented programs and serves on the Board of Directors of the Friends of the Theatre Collection of the Museum of the City of New York.

BOARD OF DIRECTORS

Richard Brandt
Jean Dalrymple
Dasha Epstein
William Gibberson
Ruth R. Goddard
Donald Grody
William Hammerstein
Jay S. Harris
Julie Harris
Radie Harris
Henry Hewes
Armina Marshall

Frederick O'Neal
Clarence A. Ross
Dore Schary
Joel Schenker
Isabelle Stevenson
Jean Stralem
Jo Sullivan
Richard Weaver
Audrey Wood

PROGRAM DIRECTOR

Wm. Spencer Reilly

ANTOINETTE PERRY AWARDS

ANTOINETTE PERRY (1888-1946)

Actress, Producer, Director, Chairman of the Board and Secretary of the American Theatre Wing. The Tony Awards were named in her honor.

The Antoinette Perry (Tony) Awards

The Tony, named in honor of Antoinette Perry, has been one of the theatre's most coveted awards and is annually bestowed on professionals for "distinguished achievement" in the theatre and not for the "best" in any category.

When Antoinette Perry died in 1946 at the age of fifty-eight, many people who knew her were determined that she would not be forgotten. As Chairman of the Board and Secretary of the American Theatre Wing throughout World War II, Antoinette Perry insisted on perfection and high standards of quality. Her dedication and tireless efforts to broaden the scope of theatre through the many programs of the American Theatre Wing affected hundreds of people.

Antoinette Perry made her first impact on the theatre in 1906, when she was only eighteen. She played opposite David Warfield in "Music Master" and, the following year, in David Belasco's "A Grand Army Man." Only two years later, and at an age when most actresses are still waiting for that first big break, Antoinette Perry retired, a star, to marry and raise a family.

Her daughters, Elaine and Margaret, pursued acting careers in the theatre. Elaine became an active member of the American Theatre Wing as well, and Margaret, who understudied Ingrid Bergman in "Liliom," stage-managed the touring production of "The Barretts of Wimpole Street."

In 1922, after the death of her husband, Antoinette Perry returned to the stage and appeared in many plays, including "Minick," by George S. Kaufman and Edna Ferber in 1924, and Margaret Anglin's 1927 production of "Electra." In association with Brock Pemberton, she then turned her talent to directing, enriching the theatre with several memorable plays, including Preston Sturges' comedy, "Strictly Dishonorable," in 1929 and Mary Chase's classic, "Harvey," in 1944.

17

When Antoinette Perry died, it was Jacob Wilk who first suggested the idea of an Antoinette Perry Memorial to John Golden. He, in turn, presented the idea to the Wing. Brock Pemberton, a long time personal friend as well as business associate, was appointed chairman of the committee, and suggested that the Wing give a series of annual awards in her name. A panel of six members was appointed to nominate candidates for the award in each category. The members who made the final selections in the first year were: Vera Allen, Louise Beck, Jane Cowl, Helen Hayes, Brooks Atkinson, Kermit Bloomgarden, Clayton Collyer, George Heller, Rudy Karnolt, Burns Mantle, Gilbert Miller, Warren P. Munsell, Solly Pernick, James E. Sauter, and Oliver Sayler.

The first awards were made at a dinner in the Grand Ballroom of the Waldorf Astoria on Easter Sunday, April 6, 1947. With Vera Allen, Antoinette Perry's successor as Wing Chairwoman, presiding, the evening included dining, dancing and a program of entertainment whose participants included Mickey Rooney, Herb Shriner, Ethel Waters and David Wayne.

The following year, Mrs. Martin Beck, one of the Wing's founders, succeeded Vera Allen as Chairwoman of the Board. When Mrs. Beck retired, the distinguished actress Helen Menken, presided in that office until 1957 when she became President of the Wing. She succeeded Helen Hayes who was elected in 1950. Until her death in 1966, Helen Menken devoted herself to the Wing and its numerous programs, including the yearly presentation of the Tony Awards. Mrs. John Stevenson, an active board member for seventeen years, was elected President and remains so today.

During the first two years, there was no official Tony award. The winners were presented with, in addition to a scroll, a cigarette lighter or a compact. The United Scenic Artists sponsored a contest for a suitable design for the award and Herman Rosse's entry, depicting the masks of comedy and tragedy on one side and the profile of Antoinette Perry on the other, was selected. In 1949, the medallion was initiated at the third annual dinner. It continues to be the official Tony® Award.

From 1947 until 1965, the dinner and Tony Award presentation was held in various ballrooms of such hotels as the Plaza, the Waldorf Astoria, and the Hotel Astor. The ceremonies were broadcast over WOR radio and The Mutual Network and, in 1956, televised for the first time on Du Mont's Channel 5. Brock Pemberton, Mrs. Martin Beck, Helen Hayes and Ilka Chase presided over the ceremonies and award presentations and entertainment was provided by such notables of the theatre as Katharine Cornell, Guthrie McClintic, Helen Hayes, Ralph Bellamy, Joan Crawford, Alfred de Liagre Jr., Gilbert Miller, Shirley Booth, Carol Channing, Joan Fontaine, Paul Newman, Geraldine Page, Anne Bancroft, Sidney Poitier, Fredric March, Robert Goulet, Gig Young, Anna Maria Alberghetti, Henry Fonda, Patricia Neal, and many others.

In spite of the death of Helen Menken in March of 1966, the awards were presented at the Rainbow Room the following month. The ceremony was subdued and, for the first and only time, held in the afternoon without public attendance or entertainment. Both factors have, since the inception of the awards up to the present day Tony ceremony, been important to the program.

Considered a vital influence in the theatre, representing quality and distinction, the League of New York Theatres was authorized by the American Theatre Wing to present the Tony Awards in 1967 when the ceremonies were moved from the traditional hotel ballroom setting to a Broadway theatre. Alexander H. Cohen produced the nationwide television show and organized the ball and supper dance after the awards. The American Theatre Wing continues to preserve the original quality of intimacy by holding a party each year at Sardi's for Wing members and friends which salutes the Tony and the Stage Door Canteen.

In 1971, Alexander H. Cohen, producer of the American Theatre Wing's Tony show, marked the twenty-fifth anniversary of the Antoinette Perry Awards. In celebration of such an auspicious event, the entertainment for that year was an extraordinary, show-stopping recapitulation of the past. David Wayne, Nanette Fabray, Alfred Drake, Ray Walston, Vivian Blaine, Sam Levene, Yul Brynner, Patricia Morison (subbing for the late Gertrude Lawrence), Edie Adams, Gwen Verdon, John Raitt, Stanley Holloway, Robert Preston, Richard Kiley, Tom Bosley, Florence Henderson (subbing for Mary Martin), Paul Lynde, Zero Mostel, Carol Channing, Angela Lansbury, Jill Hayworth, Leslie Uggams, William Daniels, Virginia Vestoff, and Lauren Bacall magically and magnificently recreated musical moments of the roles for which they had been awarded the Tony in past seasons.

VOTING

In 1947, the originating committee devised a voting system whose eligible voters were members of the Board of the American Theatre Wing, representing management, and the performer and craft unions of the entertainment field. In 1954, voting eligibility was expanded to include theatre professionals who were not members of the American Theatre Wing. Today the system has been further enlarged. Persons eligible to vote for winners of the Tony Awards, besides the Board of Directors of the American Theatre Wing, are members of the governing boards of Actors' Equity Association, the Dramatists Guild, the Society of Stage Directors and Choreographers, the United Scenic Artists, those persons whose names appear on the first and second night press lists, and the membership of the League of New York Theatres and Producers, an approximate total of 560.

Throughout the long, distinguished history of the Tony Awards, selections of nominees and winners have been executed with the principle of awarding for excellence and distinguished achievement. Although the presentations have gone through many changes, the basic principles and standards remain constant.

Categories of Awards

Play — *Award to Author; Award to Producer*
Musical — *Award to Producer*
Book of a Musical
Score *(Music and Lyrics)*
Performance by an Actor in a Play
Performance by an Actress in a Play
Performance by an Actor in a Musical
Performance by an Actress in a Musical
Performance by a Featured Actor in a Play
Performance by a Featured Actress in a Play
Performance by a Featured Actor in a Musical
Performance by a Featured Actress in a Musical
Direction of a Play
Direction of a Musical
Scenic Design
Costume Design
Lighting Design
Choreography
Special Awards

The 1940's

"In 1948, the second year that the Tony Awards were presented, I had a non-speaking part in Robinson Jeffers' "Medea," and Judith Anderson won a Tony for her brilliant performance. It was the first play I had been in on Broadway. I do not remember dreaming of such an award.

Nineteen years later I received a nomination for my performance as Julia in Edward Albee's "A Delicate Balance" (and won) and four years after that, for a leading performance in Oliver Hailey's "Father's Day" (and did not win.)

Looking back, it was the nomination that meant the most to me both times. I admired the actresses in my categories and was proud to be listed with them.

The thrill of winning lasts a minute. The memory of rehearsing, playing the parts, sharing them with audiences last much longer. And in some special way the recognition of the Tony committee makes the memories seem even dearer.

Each time I felt that the part won — the playwright won — and I accepted the Award and the scroll for them. So I treasure both and always will."

MARIAN SELDES

1947

Actors (Dramatic)
>José Ferrer, *Cyrano de Bergerac*
>Fredric March, *Years Ago*

Actresses (Dramatic)
>Ingrid Bergman, *Joan of Lorraine*
>Helen Hayes, *Happy Birthday*

Actress, Supporting or Featured (Dramatic)
>Patricia Neal, *Another Part of the Forest*

Actor, Supporting or Featured (Musical)
>David Wayne, *Finian's Rainbow*

Director
>Elia Kazan, *All My Sons*

Costumes
>Lucinda Ballard, *Happy Birthday /
>Another Part of the Forest /
>Street Scene / John Loves Mary /
>The Chocolate Soldier*
>David Ffolkes, *Henry VIII*

Choreographers
>Agnes de Mille, *Brigadoon*
>Michael Kidd, *Finian's Rainbow*

Special Awards
>Dora Chamberlain
>Mr. and Mrs. Ira Katzenberg
>Jules Leventhal
>Burns Mantle
>P. A. MacDonald
>Arthur Miller
>Vincent Sardi, Sr.
>Kurt Weill

1948

Actors (Dramatic)
>Henry Fonda, *Mister Roberts*
>Paul Kelly, *Command Decision*
>Basil Rathbone, *The Heiress*

Actresses (Dramatic)
>Judith Anderson, *Medea*
>Katharine Cornell, *Antony and*
>>*Cleopatra*
>Jessica Tandy, *A Streetcar Named Desire*

Actor (Musical)
>Paul Hartman, *Angel in the Wings*

Actress (Musical)
>Grace Hartman, *Angel in the Wings*

Play
>*Mister Roberts* by Thomas Heggen and
>>Joshua Logan/based on the
>>Thomas Heggen novel.

Producer
>Leland Hayward, *Mister Roberts*

26

Authors
Thomas Heggen and Joshua Logan,
Mister Roberts

Costumes
Mary Percy Schenck, *The Heiress*

Scenic Designer
Horace Armistead, *The Medium*

Choreographer
Jerome Robbins, *High Button Shoes*

Stage Technicians
George Gebhardt
George Pierce

Special Awards
Vera Allen, Paul Beisman, Joe E.
Brown, Robert Dowling, Experimental
Theatre, Inc., Rosamond Gilder, June
Lockhart, Mary Martin, Robert
Porterfield, James Whitmore

1949

Actor (Dramatic)
Rex Harrison, *Anne of the Thousand
Days*

Actress (Dramatic)
Martita Hunt, *The Madwoman of
Chaillot*

Actor, Supporting or Featured (Dramatic)
Arthur Kennedy, *Death of a Salesman*

Actress, Supporting or Featured (Dramatic)
Shirley Booth, *Goodbye, My Fancy*

Actor (Musical)
Ray Bolger, *Where's Charley?*

Actress (Musical)
Nanette Fabray, *Love Life*

Play
Death of a Salesman by Arthur Miller

Producers (Dramatic)
Kermit Bloomgarden and Walter Fried,
Death of a Salesman

Author
Arthur Miller, *Death of a Salesman*

Director
Elia Kazan, *Death of a Salesman*

Musical
Kiss Me Kate, music and lyrics by
Cole Porter, book by Bella and
Samuel Spewack

Producers (Musical)
Saint-Subber and Lemuel Ayers,
Kiss Me Kate

Authors (Musical)
Bella and Samuel Spewack,
Kiss Me Kate

Composer and Lyricist
Cole Porter, *Kiss Me Kate*

Costumes
>Lemuel Ayers, *Kiss Me Kate*

Scenic Designer
>Jo Mielziner, *Sleepy Hollow /
>Summer and Smoke / Anne of the
>Thousand Days / Death of a
>Salesman / South Pacific*

Choreographer
>Gower Champion, *Lend An Ear*

Conductor and Musical Director
>Max Meth, *As the Girls Go*

The 1950's

"There are two types of people. One type asserts that awards mean nothing to them. The second type breaks out into tears upon receiving an award, and thanks their mother, father, children, the producer, the director—and, if they can crowd it in—the American Baseball League.

However, I believe that people in the theatre who receive this award have a special feeling that makes them cherish the winning of a Tony. It prevents them from going on effusively. The Tony has a special value. It was created to award distinguished achievement in the theatre."

DORE SCHARY

1950

Actor (Dramatic)
Sidney Blackmer, *Come Back, Little Sheba*

Actress (Dramatic)
Shirley Booth, *Come Back, Little Sheba*

Actor (Musical)
Ezio Pinza, *South Pacific*

Actress (Musical)
Mary Martin, *South Pacific*

Actor, Supporting or Featured (Musical)
Myron McCormick, *South Pacific*

Actress, Supporting or Featured (Musical)
Juanita Hall, *South Pacific*

Play
The Cocktail Party by T. S. Eliot

Producer (Dramatic)
Gilbert Miller, *The Cocktail Party*

Author (Dramatic)
T. S. Eliot, *The Cocktail Party*

Director
Joshua Logan, *South Pacific*

Musical

South Pacific, music by Richard
Rodgers, lyrics by Oscar Hammer-
stein II, book by Oscar
Hammerstein II and Joshua Logan

Producers (Musical)

Richard Rodgers, Oscar Hammerstein
II, Leland Hayward and Joshua
Logan, *South Pacific*

Authors (Musical)

Oscar Hammerstein II and Joshua
Logan, *South Pacific*

Composer

Richard Rodgers, *South Pacific*

Costumes

Aline Bernstein, *Regina*

Scenic Designer

Jo Mielziner, *The Innocents*

Choreographer

Helen Tamiris, *Touch and Go*

Conductor and Musical Director

Maurice Abravanel, *Regina*

Stage Technician

Joe Lynn, master propertyman,
Miss Liberty

Special Awards

Maurice Evans
Mrs. Eleanor Roosevelt presented a
special award to a volunteer
worker of the American Theatre
Wing's hospital program.

1951

Actor (Dramatic)
Claude Rains, *Darkness At Noon*

Actress (Dramatic)
Uta Hagen, *The Country Girl*

Actor, Supporting or Featured (Dramatic)
Eli Wallach, *The Rose Tattoo*

Actress, Supporting or Featured (Dramatic)
Maureen Stapleton, *The Rose Tattoo*

Actor (Musical)
Robert Alda, *Guys and Dolls*

Actress (Musical)
Ethel Merman, *Call Me Madam*

Actor, Supporting or Featured (Musical)
Russell Nype, *Call Me Madam*

Actress, Supporting or Featured (Musical)
Isabel Bigley, *Guys and Dolls*

Play
The Rose Tattoo by Tennesee Williams

Producer (Dramatic)
Cheryl Crawford, *The Rose Tattoo*

Author (Dramatic)
Tennessee Williams, *The Rose Tattoo*

Director
George S. Kaufman, *Guys and Dolls.*

Musical

> *Guys and Dolls*. Music and lyrics by
> Frank Loesser, book by Jo
> Swerling and Abe Burrows

Producers (Musical)

> Cy Feuer and Ernest H. Martin,
> *Guys and Dolls*

Authors (Musical)

> Jo Swerling and Abe Burrows,
> *Guys and Dolls*

Composer and Lyricist

> Frank Loesser, *Guys and Dolls*

Costumes

> Miles White, *Bless You All*

Scenic Designer

> Boris Aronson, *The Rose Tattoo /*
> *The Country Girl / Season In*
> *The Sun*

Choreographer

> Michael Kidd, *Guys and Dolls*

Conducter and Musical Director

> Lehman Engel, *The Consul*

Stage Technician

> Richard Raven, *The Autumn Garden*

Special Award

> Ruth Green

1952

Actor (Dramatic)
 José Ferrer, *The Shrike*

Actress (Dramatic)
 Julie Harris, *I Am a Camera*

Actress (Musical)
 Gertrude Lawrence, *The King & I*

Actor (Musical)
 Phil Silvers, *Top Banana*

Actor, Supporting or Featured (Dramatic)
 John Cromwell, *Point of No Return*

Actress, Supporting or Featured (Dramatic)
 Marian Winters, *I Am a Camera*

Actor, Supporting or Featured (Musical)
 Yul Brynner, *The King & I*

Actress, Supporting or Featured (Musical)
 Helen Gallagher, *Pal Joey*

Play
 The Fourposter by Jan de Hartog

Musical
 The King & I, book and lyrics by
 Oscar Hammerstein II, music
 by Richard Rodgers

Director
 José Ferrer, *The Shrike* /
 The Fourposter / *Stalag 17*

Costumes
Irene Sharaff, *The King & I*

Scenic Designer
Jo Mielziner, *The King & I*

Choreographer
Robert Alton, *Pal Joey*

Conductor and Musical Director
Max Meth, *Pal Joey*

Stage Technician
Peter Feller, master carpenter for
Call Me Madam

Special Awards
Edward Kook
Judy Garland
Charles Boyer

1953

Actor (Dramatic)
Tom Ewell, *The Seven Year Itch*

Actress (Dramatic)
Shirley Booth, *Time of the Cuckoo*

Actor, Supporting or Featured (Dramatic)
John Williams, *Dial M for Murder*

Actress, Supporting or Featured (Dramatic)
Beatrice Straight, *The Crucible*

Actor (Musical)
Thomas Mitchell, *Hazel Flagg*

Actress (Musical)
> Rosalind Russell, *Wonderful Town*

Actor, Supporting or Featured (Musical)
> Hiram Sherman, *Two's Company*

Actress, Supporting or Featured (Musical)
> Sheila Bond, *Wish You Were Here*

Play
> *The Crucible* by Arthur Miller

Producer (Dramatic)
> Kermit Bloomgarden, *The Crucible*

Author (Dramatic)
> Arthur Miller, *The Crucible*

Director
> Joshua Logan, *Picnic*

Musical
> *Wonderful Town,* book by Joseph Fields and Jerome Chodorov, music by Leonard Bernstein, lyrics by Betty Comden and Adolph Green

Producer (Musical)
> Robert Fryer, *Wonderful Town*

Authors (Musical)
> Joseph Fields and Jerome Chodorov, *Wonderful Town*

Composer
> Leonard Bernstein, *Wonderful Town*

Costume Designer
> Miles White, *Hazel Flagg*

Scenic Designer
　　　Raoul Pène du Bois, *Wonderful Town*

Choreographer
　　　Donald Saddler, *Wonderful Town*

Conductor and Musical Director
　　　Lehman Engel, *Wonderful Town* and
　　　　Gilbert and Sullivan Season

Stage Technician
　　　Abe Kurnit, *Wish You Were Here*

Special Awards
　　　Beatrice Lillie
　　　Danny Kaye
　　　Equity Community Theatre

1954

Actor (Dramatic)
　　　David Wayne, *The Teahouse of the
　　　August Moon*

Actress (Dramatic)
　　　Audrey Hepburn, *Ondine*

Actor, Supporting or Featured (Dramatic)
　　　John Kerr, *Tea and Sympathy*

Actress, Supporting or Featured (Dramatic)
　　　Jo Van Fleet, *The Trip to Bountiful*

Actor (Musical)
　　　Alfred Drake, *Kismet*

Actress (Musical)
>> Dolores Gray, *Carnival in Flanders*

Actor, Supporting or Featured (Musical)
>> Harry Belafonte, *John Murray Anderson's Almanac*

Actress, Supporting or Featured (Musical)
>> Gwen Verdon, *Can-Can*

Play
>> *The Teahouse of the August Moon* by John Patrick

Producer (Dramatic)
>> Maurice Evans and George Schaefer, *The Teahouse of the August Moon*

Author (Dramatic)
>> John Patrick, *The Teahouse of the August Moon*

Director
>> Alfred Lunt, *Ondine*

Musical
>> *Kismet,* book by Charles Lederer and Luther Davis, music by Alexander Borodin, adapted and with lyrics by Robert Wright and George Forrest

Producer (Musical)
>> Charles Lederer, *Kismet*

Author (Musical)
>> Charles Lederer and Luther Davis, *Kismet*

Composer
> Alexander Borodin, *Kismet*

Costume Designer
> Richard Whorf, *Ondine*

Scenic Designer
>> Peter Larkin, *Ondine* and *The
>> Teahouse of the August Moon*

Choreographer
> Michael Kidd, *Can-Can*

Musical Conductor
> Louis Adrian, *Kismet*

Stage Technician
> John Davis, *Picnic*

1955

Actor (Dramatic)
> Alfred Lunt, *Quadrille*

Actress (Dramatic)
> Nancy Kelly, *The Bad Seed*

Actor, Supporting or Featured (Dramatic)
>> Francis L. Sullivan, *Witness for
>> the Prosecution*

Actress, Supporting or Featured (Dramatic)
>> Patricia Jessel, *Witness for
>> the Prosecution*

Actor (Musical)
>> Walter Slezak, *Fanny*

Actress (Musical)
>> Mary Martin, *Peter Pan*

Actor, Supporting or Featured (Musical)
>> Cyril Ritchard, *Peter Pan*

Actress, Supporting or Featured (Musical)
>> Carol Haney, *The Pajama Game*

Play
>> *The Desperate Hours* by Joseph Hayes

Producers (Dramatic)
>> Howard Erskine and Joseph Hayes,
>> *The Desperate Hours*

Author (Dramatic)
>> Joseph Hayes, *The Desperate Hours*

Director
>> Robert Montgomery, *The Desperate
>> Hours*

Musical
>> *The Pajama Game,* book by George
>> Abbott and Richard Bissell, music
>> and lyrics by Richard Adler and
>> Jerry Ross

Producers (Musical)
>> Frederick Brisson, Robert Griffith
>> and Harold S. Prince,
>> *The Pajama Game*

Authors (Musical)
>> George Abbott and Richard Bissell,
>> *The Pajama Game*

Composer and Lyricist
  Richard Adler and Jerry Ross,
    The Pajama Game

Costume Designer
  Cecil Beaton, *Quadrille*

Scenic Designer
  Oliver Messel, *House of Flowers*

Choreographer
  Bob Fosse, *The Pajama Game*

Conductor and Musical Director
  Thomas Schippers, *The Saint of
    Bleecker Street*

Stage Technician
  Richard Rodda, *Peter Pan*

Special Award
  Proscenium Productions

1956

Actor (Dramatic)
      Ben Gazzara, *A Hatful of Rain*
      Boris Karloff, *The Lark*
  * Paul Muni, *Inherit the Wind*
      Michael Redgrave, *Tiger at the Gates*
      Edward G. Robinson, *Middle of the
        Night*

Starting with 1956 our records indicate, in most cases, all the
nominees and the winner in each category. The winner is denoted
by an asterisk.

Actress (Dramatic)

    Barbara Bel Geddes, *Cat on a Hot Tin Roof*
    Gladys Cooper, *The Chalk Garden*
    Ruth Gordon, *The Matchmaker*
    * Julie Harris, *The Lark*
    Siobhan McKenna, *The Chalk Garden*
    Susan Strasberg, *The Diary of Anne Frank*

Actor, Supporting or Featured (Dramatic)

    * Ed Begley, *Inherit the Wind*
    Anthony Franciosa, *A Hatful of Rain*
    Andy Griffith, *No Time for Sergeants*
    Anthony Quayle, *Tamburlaine the Great*
    Fritz Weaver, *The Chalk Garden*

Actress, Supporting or Featured (Dramatic)

    Diane Cilento, *Tiger at the Gates*
    Anne Jackson, *Middle of the Night*
    * Una Merkel, *The Ponder Heart*
    Elaine Stritch, *Bus Stop*

Actor (Musical)

    Stephen Douglass, *Damn Yankees*
    William Johnson, *Pipe Dream*
    * Ray Walston, *Damn Yankees*

Actress (Musical)

    Carol Channing, *The Vamp*
    * Gwen Verdon, *Damn Yankees*
    Nancy Walker, *Phoenix '55*

Actor, Supporting or Featured (Musical)

    * Russ Brown, *Damn Yankees*
    Mike Kellin, *Pipe Dream*
    Will Mahoney, City Center *Finian's Rainbow*
    Scott Merrill, *The Threepenny Opera*

Actress, Supporting or Featured (Musical)
  Rae Allen, *Damn Yankees*
  Pat Carroll, *Catch a Star*
* Lotte Lenya, *The Threepenny Opera*
  Judy Tyler, *Pipe Dream*

Play

  Bus Stop by William Inge. Produced by
  Robert Whitehead and Roger
  L. Stevens
  Cat on a Hot Tin Roof by Tennessee
  Williams. Produced by The
  Playwrights' Company
* *The Diary of Anne Frank* by Frances
  Goodrich and Albert Hackett.
  Produced by Kermit Bloomgarden
  Tiger at the Gates by Jean Giraudoux,
  adapted by Christopher Fry.
  Produced by Robert L. Joseph,
  The Playwrights' Company and
  Henry M. Margolis
  The Chalk Garden by Enid Bagnold.
  Produced by Irene Mayer
  Selznick

Authors (Dramatic)
* Frances Goodrich and Albert Hackett,
  The Diary of Anne Frank

Producer (Dramatic)
* Kermit Bloomgarden, *The Diary of
  Anne Frank*

Director

  Joseph Anthony, *The Lark*
  Harold Clurman, *Bus Stop / Pipe
  Dream / Tiger at the Gates*
* Tyrone Guthrie, *The Matchmaker /
  Six Characters in Search of an
  Author / Tamburlaine the Great*

46

Garson Kanin, *The Diary of Anne Frank*
Elia Kazan, *Cat on a Hot Tin Roof*
Albert Marre, *The Chalk Garden*
Herman Shumlin, *Inherit the Wind*

Musical

* *Damn Yankees* by George Abbott and Douglass Wallop. Music by Richard Adler and Jerry Ross. Produced by Frederick Brisson, Robert Griffith, Harold S. Prince in association with Albert B. Taylor

Pipe Dream. Book and lyrics by Oscar Hammerstein II, music by Richard Rodgers. Produced by Rodgers and Hammerstein

Authors (Musical)

* George Abbott and Douglass Wallop, *Damn Yankees*

Producers (Musical)

* Frederick Brisson, Robert Griffith, Harold S. Prince in association with Albert B. Taylor, *Damn Yankees*

Composer and Lyricist

* Richard Adler and Jerry Ross, *Damn Yankees*

Conductor and Musical Director

Salvatore Dell'Isola, *Pipe Dream*
* Hal Hastings, *Damn Yankees*
Milton Rosenstock, *The Vamp*

Scenic Designer
> Boris Aronson, *The Diary of Anne Frank / Bus Stop / Once Upon a Tailor / A View from the Bridge*
> Ben Edwards, *The Ponder Heart / Someone Waiting / The Honeys*
> * Peter Larkin, *Inherit the Wind / No Time for Sergeants*
> Jo Mielziner, *Cat on a Hot Tin Roof / The Lark / Middle of the Night / Pipe Dream*
> Raymond Sovey, *The Great Sebastians*

Costume Designer
> Mainbocher, *The Great Sebastians*
> * Alvin Colt, *The Lark / Phoenix '55 / *Pipe Dream*
> Helene Pons, *The Diary of Anne Frank / Heavenly Twins / A View from the Bridge*

Choreographer
> Robert Alton, *The Vamp*
> * Bob Fosse, *Damn Yankees*
> Boris Runanin, *Phoenix '55 / Pipe Dream*
> Anna Sokolow, *Red Roses for Me*

Stage Technician
> Larry Bland, carpenter, *Middle of the Night / The Ponder Heart / Porgy and Bess*
> * Harry Green, electrician and sound man, *Middle of the Night / Damn Yankees*

Special Awards
> *The Threepenny Opera*
> The Theatre Collection of the N.Y. Public Library

48

1957

Actor (Dramatic)

  Maurice Evans, *The Apple Cart*

  Wilfred Hyde-White, *The Reluctant Debutante*

  * Fredric March, *Long Day's Journey Into Night*

  Eric Portman, *Separate Tables*

  Ralph Richardson, *The Waltz Of The Toreadors*

  Cyril Ritchard, *A Visit To A Small Planet*

Actress (Dramatic)

  Florence Eldridge, *Long Day's Journey Journey Into Night*

  * Margaret Leighton, *Separate Tables*

  Rosalind Russell, *Auntie Mame*

  Sybil Thorndike, *The Potting Shed*

Actor, Supporting or Featured (Dramatic)

  * Frank Conroy, *The Potting Shed*

  Eddie Mayehoff, *A Visit To A Small Planet*

  William Podmore, *Separate Tables*

  Jason Robards, Jr., *Long Day's Journey Into Night*

Actress, Supporting or Featured (Dramatic)

  * Peggy Cass, *Auntie Mame*

  Anna Massey, *The Reluctant Debutante*

  Beryl Measor, *Separate Tables*

  Mildred Natwick, *The Waltz Of The Toreadors*

  Phyllis Neilson-Terry, *Separate Tables*

  Diana Van Der Vlis, *The Happiest Millionaire*

49

Actor (Musical)
* Rex Harrison, *My Fair Lady*
  Fernando Lamas, *Happy Hunting*
  Robert Weede, *The Most Happy Fella*

Actress (Musical)
  Julie Andrews, *My Fair Lady*
* Judy Holiday, *Bells Are Ringing*
  Ethel Merman, *Happy Hunting*

Actor, Supporting or Featured (Musical)
* Sydney Chaplin, *Bells Are Ringing*
  Robert Coote, *My Fair Lady*
  Stanley Holloway, *My Fair Lady*

Actress, Supporting or Featured (Musical)
* Edith Adams, *Li'l Abner*
  Virginia Gibson, *Happy Hunting*
  Irra Petina, *Candide*
  Jo Sullivan, *The Most Happy Fella*

Play

* *Long Day's Journey Into Night* by
  Eugene O'Neill. Produced by
  Leigh Connell, Theodore Mann and
  José Quintero
  Separate Tables by Terence Rattigan.
  Produced by The Producers
  Theatre and Hecht-Lancaster
  The Potting Shed by Graham Greene.
  Produced by Carmen Capalbo and
  Stanley Chase
  The Waltz Of The Toreadors by
  Jean Anouilh, translated by
  Lucienne Hill. Produced by The
  Producers Theatre (Robert
  Whitehead)

Author (Dramatic)
    * Eugene O'Neill, *Long Day's Journey Into Night*

Producer (Dramatic)
    * Leigh Connell, Theodore Mann and José Quintero, *Long Day's Journey Into Night*

Director

    Joseph Anthony, *A Clearing in the Woods / The Most Happy Fella*
    Harold Clurman, *The Waltz of the Toreadors*
    Peter Glenville, *Separate Tables*
    * Moss Hart, *My Fair Lady*
    José Quintero, *Long Day's Journey Into Night*

Musical

    Bells Are Ringing. Book and lyrics by Betty Comden and Adolph Green, music by Jule Styne. Produced by The Theatre Guild
    Candide. Book by Lillian Hellman, music by Leonard Bernstein, lyrics by Richard Wilbur. Produced by Ethel Linder Reiner in association with Lester Osterman, Jr.
    * *My Fair Lady.* Book and lyrics by Alan Jay Lerner, music by Frederick Loewe. Produced by Herman Levin
    The Most Happy Fella. Book, music and lyrics by Frank Loesser. Produced by Kermit Bloomgarden and Lynn Loesser

Author (Musical)
   * Alan Jay Lerner, *My Fair Lady*

Producer (Musical)
   * Herman Levin, *My Fair Lady*

Composer
   Frederick Loewe, *My Fair Lady*

Conductor and Musical Director
   * Franz Allers, *My Fair Lady*
   Herbert Greene, *The Most Happy Fella*
   Samuel Krachmalnick, *Candide*

Scenic Designer
   Boris Aronson, *A Hole In The Head /
      Small War on Murray Hill*
   Ben Edwards, *The Waltz Of The
      Toreadors*
   George Jenkins, *The Happiest
      Millionaire / Too Late The
      Phalarope*
   Donald Oenslager, *Major Barbara*
   * Oliver Smith, *A Clearing in the
      Woods / Candide / Auntie Mame/
      *My Fair Lady / Eugenia / A
      Visit To A Small Planet*

Costume Designer
   * Cecil Beaton, *Little Glass Clock /
      My Fair Lady
   Alvin Colt, *Li'l Abner / The Sleeping
      Prince*
   Dorothy Jeakins, *Major Barbara / Too
      Late The Phalarope*
   Irene Sharaff, *Candide / Happy
      Hunting / Shangri La / Small
      War on Murray Hill*

Choreographer

        Hanya Holm, *My Fair Lady*
* Michael Kidd, *Li'l Abner*
        Dania Krupska, *The Most Happy Fella*
        Jerome Robbins and Bob Fosse, *Bells Are Ringing*

Stage Technician

        Thomas Fitzgerald, sound man, *Long Day's Journey Into Night*
        Joseph Harbach, carpenter, *Auntie Mame*
* Howard McDonald, (Posthumous), carpenter, *Major Barbara*

Special Awards

        American Shakespeare Festival
        Jean-Louis Barrault — French Repertory
        Robert Russell Bennett
        William Hammerstein
        Paul Shyre

1958

Actor (Dramatic)

* Ralph Bellamy, *Sunrise At Campobello*
        Richard Burton, *Time Remembered*
        Hugh Griffith, *Look Homeward, Angel*
        Laurence Olivier, *The Entertainer*
        Anthony Perkins, *Look Homeward, Angel*
        Peter Ustinov, *Romanoff and Juliet*
        Emlyn Williams, *A Boy Growing Up*

Actress (Dramatic)

    Wendy Hiller, *A Moon For The Misbegotten*

    Eugenie Leontovich, *The Cave Dwellers*

    * Helen Hayes, *Time Remembered*

    Siobhan McKenna, *The Rope Dancers*

    Mary Ure, *Look Back In Anger*

    Jo Van Fleet, *Look Homeward, Angel*

Actor, Supporting or Featured (Dramatic)

    * Henry Jones, *Sunrise At Campobello*

Actress, Supporting or Featured (Dramatic)

    * Anne Bancroft, *Two For The Seesaw*

Actor (Musical)

    Ricardo Montalban, *Jamaica*

    * Robert Preston, *The Music Man*

    Eddie Foy, Jr., *Rumple*

    Tony Randall, *Oh, Captain!*

Actress (Musical)

    * Thelma Ritter, *New Girl In Town*

    Lena Horne, *Jamaica*

    Beatrice Lillie, *Ziegfeld Follies*

    * Gwen Verdon, *New Girl In Town*

Actor, Supporting or Featured (Musical)

    * David Burns, *The Music Man*

Actress, Supporting or Featured (Musical)

    * Barbara Cook, *The Music Man*

Play

    The Rope Dancers by Morton Wishengrad

    Two For The Seesaw by William Gibson

Time Remembered by Jean Anouilh.
English version by Patricia Moyes
The Dark at the Top of the Stairs
by William Inge
Look Back In Anger by John Osborne
Romanoff and Juliet by Peter Ustinov
* *Sunrise At Campobello* by Dore Schary

Author (Dramatic)
* Dore Schary, *Sunrise At Campobello*

Producers (Dramatic)
* Lawrence Langner, Theresa Helburn,
Armina Marshall and Dore
Schary, *Sunrise At Compobello*

Director (Dramatic)
* Vincent J. Donchue, *Sunrise At
Campobello*

Musical

West Side Story. Book by Arthur
Laurents, music by Leonard
Bernstein, lyrics by Stephen
Sondheim
New Girl In Town. Book by George
Abbott, music and lyrics by
Bob Merrill
* *The Music Man.* Book by Meredith
Willson and Franklin Lacey,
music and lyrics by Meredith
Willson
Oh, Captain!. Book by Al Morgan and
José Ferrer, music and lyrics by
Jay Livingston and Ray Evans
Jamaica. Book by E.Y. Harburg and
Fred Saidy, music by Harold
Arlen, lyrics by E.Y. Harburg

55

Author (Musical)
> * Meredith Willson and Franklin Lacey,
> *The Music Man*

Producer (Musical)
> * Kermit Bloomgarden, Herbert Greene,
> Frank Productions, *The Music
> Man*

Composer and Lyricist
> * Meredith Willson, *The Music Man*

Conductor and Musical Director
> * Herbert Greene, *The Music Man*

Scenic Designer
> * Oliver Smith, *West Side Story*

Costume Designer
> * Motley, *The First Gentleman*

Choreographer
> * Jerome Robbins, *West Side Story*

Stage Technician
> * Harry Romar, *Time Remembered*

Special Awards
> New York Shakespeare Festival
> Mrs. Martin Beck

1959

Actor (Dramatic)
> Cedric Hardwicke, *A Majority of One*
> Alfred Lunt, *The Visit*
> Christopher Plummer, *J. B.*
> Cyril Ritchard, *The Pleasure of His
> Company*

    * Jason Robards, Jr., *The Disenchanted*
    Robert Stephens, *Epitaph for George Dillon*

Actress (Dramatic)
    * Gertrude Berg, *A Majority of One*
    Claudette Colbert, *The Marriage-Go-Round*
    Lynn Fontanne, *The Visit*
    Kim Stanley, *A Touch of the Poet*
    Maureen Stapleton, *The Cold Wind and and the Warm*

Actor, Supporting or Featured (Dramatic)
    Marc Connelly, *Tall Story*
    George Grizzard, *The Disenchanted*
    Walter Matthau, *Once More, With Feeling*
    Robert Morse, *Say, Darling*
    * Charlie Ruggles, *The Pleasure of His Company*
    George Scott, *Comes a Day*

Actress, Supporting or Featured (Dramatic)
    Maureen Delany, *God and Kate Murphy*
    Dolores Hart, *The Pleasure of His Company*
    * Julie Newmar, *The Marriage-Go-Round*
    Nan Martin, *J. B.*
    Bertrice Reading, *Requiem for a Nun*

Actor (Musical)
    Larry Blyden, *Flower Drum Song*
    * Richard Kiley, *Redhead*

Actress (Musical)
    Miyoshi Umeki, *Flower Drum Song*
    * Gwen Verdon, *Redhead*

Actor, Supporting or Featured (Musical)
* Russell Nype, *Goldilocks*
  Leonard Stone, *Redhead*
* Cast of *La Plume de Ma Tante*

Actress, Supporting or Featured (Musical)
  Julienne Marie, *Whoop-Up*
* Pat Stanley, *Goldilocks*
* Cast of *La Plume de Ma Tante*

Play

  A Touch of the Poet by Eugene
  O'Neill. Produced by The Pro-
  ducers Theatre, Robert White-
  head and Roger L. Stevens
  Epitaph for George Dillon by John
  Osborne and Anthony Creighton.
  Produced by David Merrick and
  Joshua Logan
* *J. B.* by Archibald MacLeish. Produced
  by Alfred de Liagre, Jr.
  The Disenchanted by Budd Schulberg
  and Harvey Breit. Produced by
  William Darrid and Eleanor
  Saidenberg
  The Visit by Friedrich Duerrenmatt,
  adapted by Maurice Valency.
  Produced by the Producers
  Theatre

Author (Dramatic)
  Archibald MacLeish, *J. B.*

Producer (Dramatic)
  Alfred de Liagre, Jr., *J. B.*

Director

  Peter Brook, *The Visit*
  Robert Dhéry, *La Plume de Ma Tante*

William Gaskill, *Epitaph for George Dillon*
Peter Glenville, *Rashomon*
* Elia Kazan, *J. B.*
Cyril Ritchard, *The Pleasure of His Company*
Dore Schary, *A Majority of One*

Musical

Flower Drum Song, book by Oscar Hammerstein II and Joseph Fields, lyrics by Oscar Hammerstein II, music by Richard Rodgers
La Plu:.ِ۾ de Ma Tante, written, devised and directed by Robert Dhery, music by Gerard Calvi, English lyrics by Ross Parker. (David Merrick and Joseph Kipness present the Jack Hylton Production)
* *Redhead* by Herbert and Dorothy Fields, Sidney Sheldon and David Shaw, music by Albert Hague, lyrics by Dorothy Fields

Authors (Musical)
Herbert and Dorothy Fields, Sidney Sheldon and David Shaw, *Redhead*

Producers (Musical)
Robert Fryer and Lawrence Carr, *Redhead*

Composer
Albert Hague, *Redhead*

Conductor and Musical Director
  Jay Blackston, *Redhead*
* Salvatore Dell'Isola, *Flower Drum Song*
  Lehman Engel, *Goldilocks*
  Gershon Kingsley, *La Plume de Ma Tante*

Scenic Designer
  Boris Aronson, *J. B.*
  Ballou, *The Legend of Lizzie*
  Ben Edwards, *Jane Eyre*
  Oliver Messel, *Rashomon*
* Donald Oenslager, *A Majority of One*
  Teo Otto, *The Visit*

Costume Designer
  Castillo, *Goldilocks*
  Dorothy Jeakins, *The World of Suzie Wong*
  Oliver Messel, *Rashomon*
  Irene Sharaff, *Flower Drum Song*
* Rouben Ter-Arutunian, *Redhead*

Choreographer
  Agnes de Mille, *Goldilocks*
* Bob Fosse, *Redhead*
  Carol Haney, *Flower Drum Song*
  Onna White, *Whoop-Up*

Stage Technician
  Thomas Fitzgerald, *Who Was That Lady I Saw You With?*
  Edward Flynn, *The Most Happy Fella* (City Center Revival)
* Sam Knapp, *The Music Man*

Special Awards
  John Gielgud
  Howard Lindsay and Russel Crouse

The 1960's

"There is something very special about having your work acknowledged by your peers. It is a milestone to work for, and the 'first time' something like this happens to you it is deeply satisfying."

JOEL GREY

"The curious thing about awards is that one receives them for work one does not expect to receive them for, and does not receive them for work one does. For instance, I received the Tony for "Hallelujah, Baby!"—and not for "Gypsy!" But, the Tony, which stands for excellence in the theatre is an honor whenever it comes!"

JULE STYNE

1960

Actor (Dramatic)
      * Melvyn Douglas, *The Best Man*
      Lee Tracy, *The Best Man*
      Jason Robards, Jr., *Toys in the Attic*
      Sidney Poitier, *A Raisin in the Sun*
      George C. Scott, *The Andersonville Trial*

Actress (Dramatic)
      * Anne Bancroft, *The Miracle Worker*
      Margaret Leighton, *Much Ado About Nothing*
      Claudia McNeil, *A Raisin in the Sun*
      Geraldine Page, *Sweet Bird of Youth*
      Maureen Stapleton, *Toys in the Attic*
      Irene Worth, *Toys in the Attic*

Actor, Supporting or Featured (Dramatic)
      Warren Beatty, *A Loss of Roses*
      Harry Guardino, *One More River*
     * Roddy McDowall, *The Fighting Cock*
      Rip Torn, *Sweet Bird of Youth*
      Lawrence Winters, *The Long Dream*

Actress, Supporting or Featured (Dramatic)
      Leora Dana, *The Best Man*
      Jane Fonda, *There Was a Little Girl*
      Sarah Marshall, *Goodbye, Charlie*
      Juliet Mills, *Five Finger Exercise*
     * Anne Revere, *Toys in the Attic*

Actor (Musical)
      * Jackie Gleason, *Take Me Along*
      Robert Morse, *Take Me Along*
      Walter Pidgeon, *Take Me Along*
      Andy Griffith, *Destry Rides Again*
      Anthony Perkins, *Greenwillow*

Actress (Musical)
         Carol Burnett, *Once Upon a Mattress*
         Dolores Gray, *Destry Rides Again*
         Eileen Herlie, *Take Me Along*
   * Mary Martin, *The Sound of Music*
         Ethel Merman, *Gypsy*

Actor, Supporting or Featured (Musical)
         Theodore Bikel, *The Sound of Music*
         Kurt Kasznar, *The Sound of Music*
   * Tom Bosley, *Fiorello!*
         Howard Da Silva, *Fiorello!*
         Jack Klugman, *Gypsy*

Actress, Supporting or Featured (Musical)
         Sandra Church, *Gypsy*
         Pert Kelton, *Greenwillow*
   * Patricia Neway, *The Sound of Music*
      Lauri Peters, *The Sound of Music*
         The Children, *The Sound of Music*

Play

         A Raisin in the Sun by Lorraine
            Hansberry. Produced by Philip
            Rose and David J. Cogan
         The Best Man by Gore Vidal. Produced
            by The Playwrights' Company
   * *The Miracle Worker* by William Gibson.
            Produced by Fred Coe
         The Tenth Man by Paddy Chayefsky.
            Produced by Saint-Subber and
            Arthur Cantor
         Toys in the Attic by Lillian
            Hellman. Produced by Kermit
            Bloomgarden

Author (Dramatic)
   * William Gibson, *The Miracle Worker*

Producer (Dramatic)
   * Fred Coe, *The Miracle Worker*

Director (Dramatic)

Joseph Anthony, *The Best Man*
Tyrone Guthrie, *The Tenth Man*
Elia Kazan, *Sweet Bird of Youth*
* Arthur Penn, *The Miracle Worker*
Lloyd Richards, *A Raisin in the Sun*

Musical

* *Fiorello!* by Jerome Weidman and
George Abbott. Lyrics by
Sheldon Harnick, music by Jerry
Bock. Produced by Robert E.
Griffith and Harold S. Prince
Gypsy by Arthur Laurents. Lyrics
by Stephen Sondheim, music by
Jule Styne. Produced by David
Merrick and Leland Hayward
Once Upon a Mattress, book by Jay
Thompson, Marshall Barer, Dean
Fuller, lyrics by Marshall Barer,
music by Mary Rodgers. Produced
by T. Edward Hambleton, Norris
Houghton, William and Jean
Eckart
Take Me Along. Book by Joseph
Stein and Robert Russell, lyrics
and music by Bob Merrill
* *The Sound of Music.* Book by Howard
Lindsay and Russel Crouse, lyrics
by Oscar Hammerstein II, music
by Richard Rodgers. Produced by
Leland Hayward, Richard Halliday,
Rodgers and Hammerstein

Authors (Musical)

* Jerome Weidman and George Abbott,
Fiorello!
* Howard Lindsay and Russel Crouse,
The Sound of Music

Producer (Musical)
> * Robert Griffith and Harold Prince,
>> *Fiorello!*
> * Leland Hayward and Richard Halliday,
>> *The Sound of Music*

Director (Musical)
> * George Abbott, *Fiorello!*
> Vincent J. Donehue, *The Sound of
>> Music*
> Peter Glenville, *Take Me Along*
> Michael Kidd, *Destry Rides Again*
> Jerome Robbins, *Gypsy*

Composers
> * Jerry Bock, *Fiorello!*
> * Richard Rodgers, *The Sound of Music*

Conductor and Musical Director
> Abba Bogin, *Greenwillow*
> * Frederick Dvonch, *The Sound of
>> Music*
> Lehman Engel, *Take Me Along*
> Hal Hastings, *Fiorello!*
> Milton Rosenstock, *Gypsy*

Scenic Designer (Dramatic)
> Will Steven Armstrong, *Caligula*
> * Howard Bay, *Toys in the Attic*
> David Hays, *The Tenth Man*
> George Jenkins, *The Miracle Worker*
> Jo Mielziner, *The Best Man*

Scenic Designer (Musical)
> Cecil Beaton, *Saratoga*
> William and Jean Eckart, *Fiorello!*
> Peter Larkin, *Greenwillow*
> Jo Mielziner, *Gypsy*
> * Oliver Smith, *The Sound of Music*

66

Costume Designer
    * Cecil Beaton, *Saratoga*
    Alvin Colt, *Greenwillow*
    Raoul Pène Du Bois, *Gypsy*
    Miles White, *Take Me Along*

Choreographer
    Peter Gennaro, *Fiorello!*
    * Michael Kidd, *Destry Rides Again*
    Joe Layton, *Greenwillow*
    Lee Scott, *Happy Town*
    Onna White, *Take Me Along*

Stage Technician
    Al Alloy, chief electrician, *Take Me Along*
    James Orr, chief electrician, *Greenwillow*
    * John Walters, chief carpenter, *The Miracle Worker*

Special Awards
    John D. Rockefeller 3rd
    James Thurber and Burgess Meredith, *A Thurber Carnival*

1961

Actor (Dramatic)
    Hume Cronyn, *Big Fish, Little Fish*
    Sam Levene, *The Devil's Advocate*
    * Zero Mostel, *Rhinoceros*
    Anthony Quinn, *Becket*

Actress (Dramatic)
    Tallulah Bankhead, *Midgie Purvis*
    Barbara Baxley, *Period of Adjustment*

Barbara Bel Geddes, *Mary, Mary*
* Joan Plowright, *A Taste of Honey*

Actor, Supporting or Featured (Dramatic)
Philip Bosco, *The Rape of the Belt*
Eduardo Ciannelli, *The Devil's Advocate*
* Martin Gabel, *Big Fish, Little Fish*
George Grizzard, *Big Fish, Little Fish*

Actress, Supporting or Featured (Dramatic)
* Colleen Dewhurst, *All the Way Home*
Eileen Heckart, *Invitation to a March*
Tresa Hughes, *The Devil's Advocate*
Rosemary Murphy, *Period of Adjustment*

Actor (Musical)
* Richard Burton, *Camelot*
Phil Silvers, *Do Re Mi*
Maurice Evans, *Tenderloin*

Actress (Musical)
Julie Andrews, *Camelot*
Carol Channing, *Show Girl*
* Elizabeth Seal, *Irma la Douce*
Nancy Walker, *Do Re Mi*

Actor, Supporting or Featured (Musical)
Clive Revill, *Irma la Douce*
Dick Gautier, *Bye, Bye Birdie*
Ron Husmann, *Tenderloin*
* Dick Van Dyke, *Bye, Bye Birdie*

Actress, Supporting or Featured (Musical)
Nancy Dussault, *Do Re Mi*
* Tammy Grimes, *The Unsinkable Molly Brown*
Chita Rivera, *Bye, Bye Birdie*

Play

All the Way Home by Tad Mosel.
Produced by Fred Coe in associa-
tion with Arthur Cantor
* *Becket* by Jean Anouilh, translated
by Lucienne Hill. Produced by
David Merrick
The Devil's Advocate by Dore Schary.
Produced by Dore Schary
The Hostage by Brendan Behan.
Produced by S. Field and
Caroline Burke Swann

Author (Dramatic)
* Jean Anouilh, *Becket*

Producer (Dramatic)
* David Merrick, *Becket*

Director (Dramatic)
Joseph Anthony, *Rhinoceros*
* Sir John Gielgud, *Big Fish, Little Fish*
Joan Littlewood, *The Hostage*
Arthur Penn, *All the Way Home*

Musical
* *Bye, Bye Birdie*. Book by Michael
Stewart, music by Charles Strouse,
lyrics by Lee Adams. Produced by
Edward Padula in association
with L. Slade Brown
Do Re Mi. Book by Garson Kanin,
music by Jules Styne, lyrics by
Betty Comden and Adolph Green.
Produced by David Merrick
Irma la Douce. Book and lyrics by
Alexandre Breffort, music by
Marguerite Monnot. English book
and lyrics by Julian More, David

Heneker and Monty Norman. Produced by David Merrick in association with Donald Albery and
H. M. Tennent, Ltd.

Author (Musical)
* * Michael Stewart, *Bye, Bye Birdie*

Producer (Musical)
* * Edward Padula, *Bye, Bye Birdie*

Director (Musical)
* Peter Brook, *Irma la Douce*
* * Gower Champion, *Bye, Bye Birdie*
* Garson Kanin, *Do Re Mi*

Conductor and Musical Director
* * Franz Allers, *Camelot*
* Pembroke Davenport, *13 Daughters*
* Stanley Lebowsky, *Irma la Douce*
* Elliot Lawrence, *Bye, Bye Birdie*

Scenic Designer (Dramatic)
* Roger Furse, *Duel of Angels*
* David Hays, *All the Way Home*
* Jo Mielziner, *The Devil's Advocate*
* * Oliver Smith, *Becket*
* Rouben Ter-Arutunian, *Advise and Consent*

Scenic Designer (Musical)
* George Jenkins, *13 Daughters*
* Robert Randolph, *Bye, Bye Birdie*
* * Oliver Smith, *Camelot*

Costume Designer (Dramatic)
* Theoni V. Aldredge, *The Devil's Advocate*
* * Motley, *Becket*
* Raymond Sovey, *All the Way Home*

70

Costume Designer (Musical)
 * Adrian, and Tony Duquette, *Camelot*
 Rolf Gerard, *Irma la Douce*
 Cecil Beaton, *Tenderloin*

Choreographer
 * Gower Champion, *Bye, Bye Birdie*
 Onna White, *Irma la Douce*

Stage Technician
 * Teddy Van Bemmel, *Becket*

Special Awards
 David Merrick
 The Theatre Guild

1962

Actor (Dramatic)
 Fredric March, *Gideon*
 John Mills, *Ross*
 Donald Pleasence, *The Caretaker*
 * Paul Scofield, *A Man for All Seasons*

Actress (Dramatic)
 Gladys Cooper, *A Passage to India*
 Colleen Dewhurst, *Great Day in the Morning*
 * Margaret Leighton, *Night of the Iguana*
 Kim Stanley, *A Far Country*

Actor, Supporting or Featured (Dramatic)
 Godfrey M. Cambridge, *Purlie Victorious*
 Joseph Campanella, *A Gift of Time*
 * Walter Matthau, *A Shot in the Dark*
 Paul Sparer, *Ross*

Actress, Supporting or Featured (Dramatic)
* * Elizabeth Ashley, *Take Her, She's Mine*
* Zohra Lampert, *Look: We've Come Through*
* Janet Margolin, *Daughter of Silence*
* Pat Stanley, *Sunday in New York*

Actor (Musical)
* Ray Bolger, *All American*
* Alfred Drake, *Kean*
* Richard Kiley, *No Strings*
* * Robert Morse, *How to Succeed in Business Without Really Trying*

Actress (Musical)
* * Anna Maria Alberghetti, *Carnival*
* * Diahann Carroll, *No Strings*
* Molly Picon, *Milk and Honey*
* Elaine Stritch, *Sail Away*

Actor, Supporting or Featured (Musical)
* Orson Bean, *Subways Are for Sleeping*
* Severn Darden, *From the Second City*
* Pierre Olaf, *Carnival*
* * Charles Nelson Reilly, *How to Succeed . . .*

Actress, Supporting or Featured (Musical)
* Elizabeth Allen, *The Gay Life*
* Barbara Harris, *From the Second City*
* * Phyllis Newman, *Subways Are for Sleeping*
* Barbra Streisand, *I Can Get It for You Wholesale*

Play

* *A Man for All Seasons* by Robert Bolt. Produced by Robert Whitehead and Roger L. Stevens

Gideon by Paddy Chayefsky. Produced
by Fred Coe and Arthur Cantor

The Caretaker by Harold Pinter.
Produced by Roger L. Stevens,
Frederick Brisson and Gilbert
Miller
The Night of the Iguana by
Tennessee Williams. Produced by
Charles Bowden and Viola Rubber

Author (Dramatic)
* Robert Bolt, *A Man for All Seasons*

Producer (Dramatic)
Charles Bowden and Viola Rubber,
Night of the Iguana
Fred Coe and Arthur Cantor, *Gideon*
David Merrick, *Ross*
* Robert Whitehead and Roger L.
Stevens, *A Man for All Seasons*

Director (Dramatic)
Tyrone Guthrie, *Gideon*
Donald McWhinnie, *The Caretaker*
José Quintero, *Great Day in the
Morning*
* Noel Willman, *A Man for All Seasons*

Musical

Carnival. Book by Michael Stewart
and Helen Deutsch, music and
lyrics by Bob Merrill. Produced
by David Merrick
* *How to Succeed in Business Without
Really Trying,* book by Abe
Burrows, Jack Weinstock and
Willie Gilbert, music and lyrics
by Frank Loesser. Produced by

73

Cy Feuer and Ernest Martin.
Milk and Honey. Book by Don Appell,
lyrics and music by Jerry
Herman. Produced by Gerard
Oestreicher.
No Strings. Book by Samuel Taylor,
music and lyrics by Richard
Rodgers. Produced by Richard
Rodgers in association with
Samuel Taylor.

Author (Musical)
     * Abe Burrows, Jack Weinstock and
       Willie Gilbert, *How to
       Succeed* . . .
       Michael Stewart and Helen Deutsch,
       Carnival

Producer (Musical)
       Helen Bonfils, Haila Stoddard and
         Charles Russell, *Sail Away*
    * Cy Feuer and Ernest Martin, *How to
       Succeed* . . .
       David Merrick, *Carnival*
       Gerard Oestreicher, *Milk and Honey*

Director (Musical)
     * Abe Burrows, *How to Succeed* . . .
       Gower Champion, *Carnival*
       Joe Layton, *No Strings*
       Joshua Logan, *All American*

Composer
       Richard Adler, *Kwamina*
       Jerry Herman, *Milk and Honey*
       Frank Loesser, *How to Succeed* . . .
    * Richard Rodgers, *No Strings*

Conductor and Musical Director
Pembroke Davenport, *Kean*
Herbert Greene, *The Gay Life*
* Elliot Lawrence, *How to Succeed* . . .
Peter Matz, *No Strings*

Scenic Designer
* Will Steven Armstrong, *Carnival*
Rouben Ter-Arutunian, *A Passage
to India*
David Hays, *No Strings*
Oliver Smith, *The Gay Life*

Costume Designer
* Lucinda Ballard, *The Gay Life*
Donald Brooks, *No Strings*
Motley, *Kwamina*
Miles White, *Milk and Honey*

Choreographer
* Agnes de Mille, *Kwamina*
Michael Kidd, *Subways Are for
Sleeping*
Dania Krupska, *The Happiest Girl
in the World*
* Joe Layton, *No Strings*

Stage Technician
Al Alloy, *Ross*
* Michael Burns, *A Man for All Seasons*

Special Awards
Brooks Atkinson
Franco Zeffirelli
Richard Rodgers
Richard Rodgers also received the
Tony for "*No Strings*"

1963

Actor (Dramatic)
> Charles Boyer, *Lord Pengo*
> Paul Ford, *Never Too Late*
> * Arthur Hill, *Who's Afraid of Virginia Woolf?*
> Bert Lahr, *The Beauty Part*

Actress (Dramatic)
> Hermione Baddeley, *The Milk Train Doesn't Stop Here Anymore*
> * Uta Hagen, *Who's Afraid of Virginia Woolf?*
> Margaret Leighton, *Tchin-Tchin*
> Claudia McNeill, *Tiger Tiger Burning Bright*

Actor, Supporting or Featured (Dramatic)
> * Alan Arkin, *Enter Laughing*
> Barry Gordon, *A Thousand Clowns*
> Paul Rogers, *Photo Finish*
> Frank Silvera, *The Lady of the Camellias*

Actress, Supporting or Featured (Dramatic)
> * Sandy Dennis, *A Thousand Clowns*
> Melinda Dillon, *Who's Afraid of Virginia Woolf?*
> Alice Ghostley, *The Beauty Part*
> Zohra Lampert, *Mother Courage and Her Children*

Actor (Musical)
> Sid Caesar, *Little Me*
> * Zero Mostel, *A Funny Thing Happened on the Way to the Forum*

Anthony Newley, *Stop the World —
I Want to Get Off*
Clive Revill, *Oliver!*

Actress (Musical)
Georgia Brown, *Oliver!*
Nanette Fabray, *Mr. President*
Sally Ann Howes, *Brigadoon*
* Vivien Leigh, *Tovarich*

Actor, Supporting or Featured (Musical)
* David Burns, *A Funny Thing Happened
on the Way to the Forum*
Jack Gilford, *A Funny Thing
Happened on the Way to the
Forum*
David Jones, *Oliver!*
Swen Swenson, *Little Me*

Actress, Supporting or Featured (Musical)
Ruth Kobart, *A Funny Thing
Happened on the Way to the
Forum*
Virginia Martin, *Little Me*
* Anna Quayle, *Stop the World — I
Want to Get Off*
Louise Troy, *Tovarich*

Play

A Thousand Clowns by Herb Gardner.
Produced by Fred Coe and Arthur
Cantor
Mother Courage and Her Children by
Bertolt Brecht, adapted by Eric
Bentley. Produced by Cheryl
Crawford and Jerome Robbins
Tchin-Tchin by Sidney Michaels.
Produced by David Merrick.

* *Who's Afraid of Virginia Woolf?* by
Edward Albee. Produced by
Theatre 1963, Richard Barr and
Clinton Wilder

Producer (Dramatic)
The Actors Studio Theatre, *Strange
Interlude*
* Richard Barr and Clinton Wilder,
Theatre 1963, *Who's Afraid of
Virginia Woolf?*
Cheryl Crawford and Jerome Robbins,
*Mother Courage and Her
Children*
Paul Vroom, Buff Cobb and Burry
Fredrik, *Too True To Be Good*

Director (Dramatic)
George Abbott, *Never Too Late*
John Gielgud, *The School for
Scandal*
Peter Glenville, *Tchin-Tchin*
* Alan Schneider, *Who's Afraid of
Virginia Woolf?*

Musical
* *A Funny Thing Happened on the
Way to the Forum.* Book by
Burt Shevelove and Larry
Gelbart, music and lyrics by
Stephen Sondheim. Produced by
Harold Prince
Little Me. Book by Neil Simon,
music by Cy Coleman, lyrics by
Carolyn Leigh. Produced by Cy
Feuer and Ernest Martin
Oliver!. Book, music and lyrics by
Lionel Bart. Produced by David
Merrick and Donald Albery

78

Stop the World — I Want to Get Off. Book, music and lyrics by Leslie Bricusse and Anthony Newley. Produced by David Merrick in association with Bernard Delfont

Author (Musical)

Lionel Bart, *Oliver!*

Leslie Bricusse and Anthony Newley, *Stop the World — I Want to Get Off*

* Burt Shevelove and Larry Gelbart, *A Funny Thing Happened on the Way to the Forum*

Neil Simon, *Little Me*

Producer (Musical)

Cy Feuer and Ernest Martin, *Little Me*

David Merrick and Donald Albery, *Oliver!*

* Harold Prince, *A Funny Thing Happened on the Way to the Forum*

Director (Musical)

* George Abbott, *A Funny Thing Happened Happened on the Way to the Forum*

Peter Coe, *Oliver!*

John Fearnley, *Brigadoon*

Cy Feuer and Bob Fosse, *Little Me*

Composer and Lyricist

* Lionel Bart, *Oliver!*

Leslie Bricusse and Anthony Newley, *Stop the World — I Want to Get Off*

Cy Coleman and Carolyn Leigh, *Little Me*

Milton Schafer and Ronny Graham, *Bravo Giovanni*

Conductor and Musical Director
    Jay Blackton, *Mr. President*
    Anton Coppola, *Bravo Giovanni*
  * Donald Pippin, *Oliver!*
    Julius Rudel, *Brigadoon*

Scenic Designer
    Will Steven Armstrong, *Tchin-Tchin*
  * Sean Kenny, *Oliver!*
    Anthony Powell, *The School for Scandal*
    Franco Zeffirelli, *The Lady of the Camellias*

Costume Designer
    Marcel Escoffier, *The Lady of the Camellias*
    Robert Fletcher, *Little Me*
    Motley, *Mother Courage and Her Children*
  * Anthony Powell, *The School for Scandal*

Choreographer
  * Bob Fosse, *Little Me*
    Carol Haney, *Bravo Giovanni*

Stage Technician
  * Solly Pernick, *Mr. President*
    Milton Smith, *Beyond the Fringe*

Special Awards
    W. McNeil Lowry
    Irving Berlin
    Alan Bennett
    Peter Cook
    Jonathan Miller
    Dudley Moore

1964

Actor (Dramatic)
        Richard Burton, *Hamlet*
        Albert Finney, *Luther*
    * Alec Guinness, *Dylan*
        Jason Robards, Jr, *After the Fall*

Actress (Dramatic) Play
        Elizabeth Ashley, *Barefoot in the
            Park*
    * Sandy Dennis, *Any Wednesday*
        Colleen Dewhurst, *The Ballad of the
            Sad Café*
        Julie Harris, *Marathon '33*

Actor, Supporting or Featured (Dramatic)
        Lee Allen, *Marathon '33*
    * Hume Cronyn, *Hamlet*
        Michael Dunn, *The Ballad of the Sad
            Café*
        Larry Gates, *A Case of Libel*

Actress, Supporting or Featured (Dramatic)
    * Barbara Loden, *After the Fall*
        Rosemary Murphy, *Any Wednesday*
        Kate Reid, *Dylan*
        Diana Sands, *Blues for Mister Charlie*

Actor (Musical)
        Sydney Chaplin, *Funny Girl*
        Bob Fosse, *Pal Joey* (City
            Center revival)
    * Bert Lahr, *Foxy*
        Steve Lawrence, *What Makes Sammy
            Run*

Actress (Musical)
* * Carol Channing, *Hello, Dolly!*
* Beatrice Lillie, *High Spirits*
* Barbra Streisand, *Funny Girl*
* Inga Swenson, *110 in the Shade*

Actor, Supporting or Featured (Musical)
* * Jack Cassidy, *She Loves Me*
* Will Geer, *110 in the Shade*
* Danny Meehan, *Funny Girl*
* Charles Nelson Reilly, *Hello, Dolly!*

Actress, Supporting or Featured (Musical)
* Julienne Marie, *Foxy*
* Kay Medford, *Funny Girl*
* * Tessie O'Shea, *The Girl Who Came to Supper*
* Louise Troy, *High Spirits*

Play

The Ballad of the Sad Café by Edward Albee. Produced by Lewis Allen and Ben Edwards
Barefoot in the Park by Neil Simon. Produced by Saint Subber
Dylan by Sidney Michaels. Produced by George W. George and Frank Granat
* *Luther* by John Osborne. Produced by David Merrick

Author (Dramatic)
John Osborne, *Luther*

Producer (Dramatic)
Lewis Allen and Ben Edwards, *The Ballad of the Sad Café*

George W. George and Frank Granat,
Dylan
* Herman Shumlin, *The Deputy*
Saint Subber, *Barefoot in the Park*

Director (Dramatic)
June Havoc, *Marathon '33*
* Mike Nichols, *Barefoot in the Park*
Alan Schneider, *The Ballad of the
Sad Café*
Herman Shumlin, *The Deputy*

Musical

Funny Girl. Book by Isobel Lennart,
music by Jule Styne, lyrics by
Bob Merrill. Produced by Ray
Stark
* *Hello, Dolly!* Book by Michael
Stewart, music and lyrics by
Jerry Herman. Produced by
David Merrick
High Spirits. Book, lyrics and music
by Hugh Martin and Timothy
Gray. Produced by Lester Oster-
man, Robert Fletcher and
Richard Horner
She Loves Me. Book by Joe Masteroff,
music by Jerry Bock, lyrics by
Sheldon Harnick. Produced by
Harold Prince in association
with Lawrence N. Kasha and
Philip C. McKenna

Author (Musical)
Noel Coward and Harry Kurnitz, *The
Girl Who Came To Supper*
Joe Masteroff, *She Loves Me*
Hugh Martin and Timothy Gray, *High
Spirits*
* Michael Stewart, *Hello, Dolly!*

Producer (Musical)
    City Center Light Opera Company,
      West Side Story
  * David Merrick, *Hello, Dolly!*
    Harold Prince, *She Loves Me*
    Ray Stark, *Funny Girl*

Director (Musical)
    Joseph Anthony, *110 in the Shade*
  * Gower Champion, *Hello, Dolly!*
    Noel Coward, *High Spirits*
    Harold Prince, *She Loves Me*

Composer and Lyricist
  * Jerry Herman, *Hello, Dolly!*
    Hugh Martin and Timothy Gray, *High
      Spirits*
    Harvey Schmidt and Tom Jones, *110
      in the Shade*
    Jule Styne and Bob Merrill, *Funny
      Girl*

Conductor and Musical Director
  * Shepard Coleman, *Hello, Dolly!*
    Lehman Engel, *What Makes Sammy
      Run?*
    Charles Jaffe, *West Side Story*
    Fred Werner, *High Spirits*

Scenic Designer
    Raoul Pène Du Bois, *The Student
      Gypsy*
    Ben Edwards, *The Ballad of the Sad
      Café*
    David Hays, *Marco Millions*
  * Oliver Smith, *Hello, Dolly!*

Costume Designer
Irene Sharaff, *The Girl Who Came To Supper*
Beni Montresor, *Marco Millions*
Rouben Ter-Arutunian, *Arturo Ui*
* Freddy Wittop, *Hello, Dolly!*

Choreographer
* Gower Champion, *Hello, Dolly!*
Danny Daniels, *High Spirits*
Carol Haney, *Funny Girl*
Herbert Ross, *Anyone Can Whistle*

Special Award
Eva Le Gallienne

1965

Actor (Dramatic)
John Gielgud, *Tiny Alice*
* Walter Matthau, *The Odd Couple*
Donald Pleasence, *Poor Bitos*
Jason Robards, *Hughie*

Actress (Dramatic)
Marjorie Rhodes, *All In Good Time*
Bea Richards, *The Amen Corner*
Diana Sands, *The Owl and the Pussycat*
* Irene Worth, *Tiny Alice*

Actor, Supporting or Featured (Dramatic)
* Jack Albertson, *The Subject Was Roses*
Murray Hamilton, *Absence of a Cello*
Martin Sheen, *The Subject Was Roses*
Clarence Williams III, *Slow Dance on the Killing Ground*

Actress, Supporting or Featured (Dramatic)
Rae Allen, *Traveller Without Luggage*
Alexandra Berlin, *All In Good Time*
Carolan Daniels, *Slow Dance on the Killing Ground*
* Alice Ghostley, *The Sign in Sidney Brustein's Window*

Actor (Musical)
Sammy Davis, *Golden Boy*
* Zero Mostel, *Fiddler On The Roof*
Cyril Ritchard, *The Roar of the Greasepaint — The Smell of the Crowd*
Tommy Steele, *Half A Sixpence*

Actress (Musical)
Elizabeth Allen, *Do I Hear A Waltz?*
Nancy Dussault, *Bajour*
* Liza Minnelli, *Flora, the Red Menace*
Inga Swenson, *Baker Street*

Actor, Supporting or Featured (Musical)
Jack Cassidy, *Fade Out — Fade In*
James Grout, *Half A Sixpence*
* Victor Spinetti, *Oh, What A Lovely War*
Jerry Orbach, *Guys and Dolls*

Actress, Supporting or Featured (Musical)
 * Maria Karnilova, *Fiddler On The Roof*
 Luba Lisa, *I Had A Ball*
 Carrie Nye, *Half A Sixpence*
 Barbara Windsor, *Oh, What A Lovely War*

Play
 Luv by Murray Schisgal. Produced by Claire Nichtern
 The Odd Couple by Neil Simon. Produced by Saint-Subber
 * *The Subject Was Roses* by Frank Gilroy. Produced by Edgar Lansbury
 Tiny Alice by Edward Albee. Produced by Theatre 1965, Richard Barr, Clinton Wilder

Author (Dramatic)
 Edward Albee, *Tiny Alice*
 Frank Gilroy, *The Subject Was Roses*
 Murray Schisgal, *Luv*
 * Neil Simon, *The Odd Couple*

Producer (Dramatic)
 Hume Cronyn, Allen-Hogdon Inc., Stevens Productions Inc., Bonfils-Seawell Enterprises, *Slow Dance on the Killing Ground*
 * Claire Nichtern, *Luv*
 Theatre 1965, Richard Barr, Clinton Wilder, *Tiny Alice*
 Robert Whitehead, *Tartuffe*

Director (Dramatic)
 William Ball, *Tartuffe*
 Ulu Grosbard, *The Subject Was Roses*
 * Mike Nichols, *Luv* and *The Odd Couple*
 Alan Schneider, *Tiny Alice*

Musical

* *Fiddler On The Roof.* Book by Joseph Stein, music by Jerry Bock, lyrics by Sheldon Harnick. Produced by Harold Prince

Golden Boy. Book by Clifford Odets and William Gibson, music by Charles Strouse, lyrics by Lee Adams. Produced by Hillard Elkins

Half A Sixpence. Book by Beverly Cross, music and lyrics by David Heneker. Produced by Allen Hodgdon, Stevens Productions and Harold Fielding

Oh, What A Lovely War. Devised by Joan Littlewood for Theatre Workshop, Charles Chilton and Members of the Cast. Produced by David Merrick and Gerry Raffles

Author (Musical)

Jerome Coopersmith, *Baker Street*
Beverly Cross, *Half A Sixpence*
Sidney Michaels, *Ben Franklin In Paris*
* Joseph Stein, *Fiddler On The Roof*

Producer (Musical)

Allen-Hodgdon, Stevens Productions and Harold Fielding, *Half A Sixpence*
Hillard Elkins, *Golden Boy*
David Merrick, *The Roar of the Greasepaint — The Smell of the Crowd*
* Harold Prince, *Fiddler On The Roof*

88

Director (Musical)

    Joan Littlewood, *Oh, What A Lovely War*

    Anthony Newley, *The Roar of the Greasepaint — The Smell of the Crowd*

* Jerome Robbins, *Fiddler On The Roof*

    Gene Saks, *Half A Sixpence*

Composer and Lyricist

* Jerry Bock and Sheldon Harnick, *Fiddler On The Roof*

    Leslie Bricusse and Anthony Newley, *The Roar of the Greasepaint — The Smell of the Crowd*

    David Heneker, *Half A Sixpence*

    Richard Rodgers and Stephen Sondheim, *Do I Hear A Waltz?*

Scenic Designer

    Boris Aronson, *Fiddler On The Roof* and *Incident At Vichy*

    Sean Kenny, *The Roar of the Greasepaint — The Smell of the Crowd*

    Beni Montresor, *Do I Hear A Waltz?*

* Oliver Smith, **Baker Street, Luv* and *The Odd Couple*

Costume Designer

    Jane Greenwood, *Tartuffe*

    Motley, *Baker Street*

    Freddy Wittop, *The Roar of the Greasepaint — The Smell of the Crowd*

* Patricia Zipprodt, *Fiddler On The Roof*

Choreographer

    Peter Gennaro, *Bajour*

    Donald McKayle, *Golden Boy*

* Jerome Robbins, *Fiddler On The Roof*

    Onna White, *Half A Sixpence*

Special Awards
> Gilbert Miller
> Oliver Smith

1966

Actor (Dramatic)
> Roland Culver, *Ivanov*
> Donald Donnelly and Patrick Bedford,
>   *Philadelphia, Here I Come!*
> * Hal Holbrook, *Mark Twain Tonight!*
> Nicol Williamson, *Inadmissible*
>   *Evidence*

Actress (Dramatic)
> Sheila Hancock, *Entertaining Mr.*
>   *Sloan*
> * Rosemary Harris, *The Lion in Winter*
> Kate Reid, *Slapstick Tragedy*
> Lee Remick, *Wait Until Dark*

Actor, Supporting or Featured (Dramatic)
> Burt Brinckerhoff, *Cactus Flower*
> A. Larry Haines, *Generation*
> Eamon Kelly, *Philadelphia*
> * Patrick Magee, *Marat/Sade*

Actress, Supporting or Featured (Dramatic)
> * Zoe Caldwell, *Slapstick Tragedy*
> Glenda Jackson, *Marat/Sade*
> Mairin D. O'Sullivan, *Philadelphia*
> Brenda Vaccaro, *Cactus Flower*

Actor (Musical)
> Jack Cassidy, *Superman*
> John Cullum, *On A Clear Day You*
>   *Can See Forever*
> * Richard Kiley, *Man of La Mancha*
> Harry Secombe, *Pickwick*

Actress (Musical)
  Barbara Harris, *On A Clear Day*
  Julie Harris, *Skyscraper*
  * Angela Lansbury, *Mame*
  Gwen Verdon, *Sweet Charity*

Actor, Supporting or Featured (Musical)
  Roy Castle, *Pickwick*
  John McMartin, *Sweet Charity*
  * Frankie Michaels, *Mame*
  Michael O'Sullivan, *Superman*

Actress, Supporting or Featured (Musical)
  * Beatrice Arthur, *Mame*
  Helen Gallagher, *Sweet Charity*
  Patricia Marand, *Superman*
  Charlotte Rae, *Pickwick*

Play
  Inadmissible Evidence by John
    Osborne. Produced by the David
    Merrick Arts Foundation
  * *Marat/Sade* by Peter Weiss. English
    version by Geoffrey Skelton.
    Produced by the David Merrick
    Arts Foundation
  Philadelphia, Here I Come! by
    Brian Friel. Produced by the
    David Merrick Arts Foundation
  The Right Honourable Gentleman by
    Michael Dyne. Produced by Peter
    Cookson, Amy Lynn and Walter
    Schwimmer

Director (Dramatic)
  * Peter Brook, *Marat/Sade*
  Hilton Edwards, *Philadelphia*
  Ellis Rabb, *You Can't Take It With
    You*
  Noel Willman, *The Lion in Winter*

Musical

> *Mame.* Book by Jerome Lawrence and
> Robert E. Lee, music and lyrics
> by Jerry Herman. Produced by
> Sylvia and Joseph Harris, Robert
> Fryer and Lawrence Carr
>
> * *Man of La Mancha.* Book by Dale
> Wasserman, music by Mitch Leigh,
> lyrics by Joe Darion. Produced
> by Albert W. Selden and Hal
> James
>
> *Skyscraper.* Book by Peter Stone,
> music by James Van Heusen,
> lyrics by Sammy Cahn. Produced
> by Cy Feuer and Ernest M.
> Martin
>
> *Sweet Charity.* Book by Neil Simon,
> music by Cy Coleman, lyrics by
> Dorothy Fields. Produced by
> Sylvia and Joseph Harris, Robert
> Fryer and Lawrence Carr

Director (Musical)

> Cy Feuer, *Skyscraper*
> Bob Fosse, *Sweet Charity*
> * Albert Marre, *Man of La Mancha*
> Gene Saks, *Mame*

Composer and Lyricist

> Cy Coleman and Dorothy Fields,
> *Sweet Charity*
> Jerry Herman, *Mame*
> * Mitch Leigh and Joe Darion, *Man of
> La Mancha*
> Burton Lane and Alan Jay Lerner, *On
> A Clear Day*

Scenic Designer
* Howard Bay, *Man of La Mancha*
  William and Jean Eckart, *Mame*
  David Hays, *Drat! The Cat!*
  Robert Randolph, *Anya, Skyscraper*
  and *Sweet Charity*

Costume Designer
  Loudon Sainthill, *The Right
  Honourable Gentleman*
  Howard Bay and Patton Campbell,
  Man of La Mancha
  Irene Sharaff, *Sweet Charity*
* Gunilla Palmstierna-Weiss, *Marat/Sade*

Choreographer
  Jack Cole, *Man of La Mancha*
* Bob Fosse, *Sweet Charity*
  Michael Kidd, *Skyscraper*
  Onna White, *Mame*

Special Award
  Helen Menken (posthumous)

1967

Actor (Dramatic)
  Hume Cronyn, *A Delicate Balance*
  Donald Madden, *Black Comedy*
  Donald Moffat, *Right You Are* and
  The Wild Duck
* Paul Rogers, *The Homecoming*

Actress (Dramatic)
  Eileen Atkins, *The Killing of Sister
  George*

Vivien Merchant, *The Homecoming*
Rosemary Murphy, *A Delicate Balance*
* Beryl Reid, *The Killing of Sister George*

Actor, Supporting or Featured (Dramatic)
Clayton Corzatte, *The School for Scandal*
Stephen Elliott, *Marat/Sade*
* Ian Holm, *The Homecoming*
Sydney Walker, *The Wild Duck*

Actress, Supporting or Featured (Dramatic)
Camila Ashland, *Black Comedy*
Brenda Forbes, *The Loves of Cass McGuire*
* Marian Seldes, *A Delicate Balance*
Maria Tucci, *The Rose Tattoo*

Actor (Musical)
Alan Alda, *The Apple Tree*
Jack Gilford, *Cabaret*
* Robert Preston, *I Do! I Do!*
Norman Wisdom, *Walking Happy*

Actress (Musical)
* Barbara Harris, *The Apple Tree*
Lotte Lenya, *Cabaret*
Mary Martin, *I Do! I Do!*
Louise Troy, *Walking Happy*

Actor, Supporting or Featured (Musical)
Leon Bibb, *A Hand is on the Gate*
Gordon Dilworth, *Walking Happy*
* Joel Grey, *Cabaret*
Edward Winter, *Cabaret*

Actress, Supporting or Featured (Musical)
* Peg Murray, *Cabaret*
Leland Palmer, *A Joyful Noise*

94

Josephine Premice, *A Hand is on
the Gate*
Susan Watson, *A Joyful Noise*

Play

A Delicate Balance, by Edward Albee.
Produced by Theatre 1967,
Richard Barr and Clinton Wilder
Black Comedy, by Peter Shaffer.
Produced by Alexander H. Cohen
* *The Homecoming,* by Harold Pinter.
Produced by Alexander H. Cohen
The Killing of Sister George by
Frank Marcus. Produced by Helen
Bonfils and Morton Gottlieb

Director (Dramatic)

John Dexter, *Black Comedy*
Donald Driver, *Marat/Sade*
* Peter Hall, *The Homecoming*
Alan Schneider, *A Delicate Balance*

Musical

* *Cabaret.* Book by Joe Masteroff,
music by John Kander, lyrics by
Fred Ebb. Produced by Harold
Prince in association with Ruth
Mitchell
I Do! I Do! Book and lyrics by
Tom Jones, music by Harvey
Schmidt. Produced by David
Merrick
The Apple Tree. Book by Sheldon
Harnick and Jerry Bock, music
by Jerry Bock, lyrics by Sheldon
Harnick. Produced by Stuart
Ostrow

95

Walking Happy. Book by Roger O. Hirson and Ketti Frings, music by James Van Heusen, lyrics by Sammy Cahn. Produced by Cy Feuer and Ernest M. Martin

Director (Musical)
Gower Champion, *I Do! I Do!*
Mike Nichols, *The Apple Tree*
Jack Sydow, *Annie Get Your Gun*
* Harold Prince, *Cabaret*

Composer and Lyricist
Jerry Bock and Sheldon Harnick, *The Apple Tree*
Sammy Cahn and James Van Heusen, *Walking Happy*
Tom Jones and Harvey Schmidt, *I Do! I Do!*
* John Kander and Fred Ebb, *Cabaret*

Scene Designer
* Boris Aronson, *Cabaret*
John Bury, *The Homecoming*
Oliver Smith, *I Do! I Do!*
Alan Tagg, *Black Comedy*

Choreographer
Michael Bennett, *A Joyful Noise*
Danny Daniels, *Walking Happy* and *Annie Get Your Gun*
* Ronald Field, *Cabaret*
Lee Theodore, *The Apple Tree*

Costume Designer
Nancy Potts, *The Wild Duck* and *The School for Scandal*
Tony Walton, *The Apple Tree*
Freddy Wittop, *I Do! I Do!*
* Patricia Zipprodt, *Cabaret*

1968

Actor (Dramatic)
    * Martin Balsam, *You Know I Can't Hear You When the Water's Running*
       Albert Finney, *Joe Egg*
       Milo O'Shea, *Staircase*
       Alan Webb, *I Never Sang for My Father*

Actress (Dramatic)
    * Zoe Caldwell, *The Prime of Miss Jean Brodie*
       Colleen Dewhurst, *More Stately Mansions*
       Maureen Stapleton, *Plaza Suite*
       Dorothy Tutin, *Portrait of a Queen*

Actor, Supporting or Featured (Dramatic)
       Paul Hecht, *Rosencrantz and Guildenstern Are Dead*
       Brian Murray, *Rosencrantz and Guildenstern Are Dead*
    * James Patterson, *The Birthday Party*
       John Wood, *Rosencrantz and Guildenstern Are Dead*

Actress, Supporting or Featured (Dramatic)
       Pert Kelton, *Spofford*
    * Zena Walker, *Joe Egg*
       Ruth White, *The Birthday Party*
       Eleanor Wilson, *Weekend*

Actor (Musical)
    * Robert Goulet, *The Happy Time*
       Robert Hooks, *Hallelujah, Baby!*
       Anthony Roberts, *How Now, Dow Jones*
       David Wayne, *The Happy Time*

Actress (Musical)
        Melina Mercouri, *Illya Darling*
  * Patricia Routledge, *Darling of the Day*
  * Leslie Uggams, *Hallelujah, Baby!*
        Brenda Vaccaro, *How Now, Dow Jones*

Actor, Supporting or Featured (Musical)
        Scott Jacoby, *Golden Rainbow*
        Nikos Kourkoulos, *Illya Darling*
        Mike Rupert, *The Happy Time*
  * Hiram Sherman, *How Now, Dow Jones*

Actress, Supporting or Featured (Musical)
        Geula Gill, *The Grand Music Hall of Israel*
        Julie Gregg, *The Happy Time*
  * Lillian Hayman, *Hallelujah, Baby!*
        Alice Playten, *Henry, Sweet Henry*

Play

        Joe Egg, by Peter Nichols. Produced by Joseph Cates and Henry Fownes
        Plaza Suite, by Neil Simon. Produced by Saint-Subber
  * *Rosencrantz and Guildenstern Are Dead,* by Tom Stoppard. Produced by The David Merrick Arts Foundation
        The Price, by Arthur Miller. Produced by Robert Whitehead

Producer (Dramatic)
  * David Merrick Arts Foundation, *Rosencrantz and Guildenstern Are Dead*

Director (Dramatic)

> Michael Blakemore, *Joe Egg*
> Derek Goldby, *Rosencrantz and Guildenstern Are Dead*
> * Mike Nichols, *Plaza Suite*
> Alan Schneider, *You Know I Can't Hear You When the Water's Running*

Musical

> * *Hallelujah, Baby!* Book by Arthur Laurents, music by Jule Styne, Lyrics by Betty Comden and Adolph Green. Produced by Albert Selden, Hal James, Jane C. Nusbaum, and Harry Rigby
> *The Happy Time.* Book by N. Richard Nash, Music by John Kander, lyrics by Fred Ebb. Produced by David Merrick
> *How Now, Dow Jones.* Book by Max Shulman, music by Elmer Bernstein, lyrics by Carolyn Leigh. Produced by David Merrick
> *Illya, Darling.* Book by Jules Dassin, music by Manos Hadjidakis, lyrics by Joe Darion. Produced by Kermit Bloomgarden

Producer (Musical)

> * Albert Selden, Hal James, Jane C. Nusbaum and Harry Rigby, *Hallelujah, Baby!*

Director (Musical)

> George Abbott, *How Now, Dow Jones*
> * Gower Champion, *The Happy Time*
> Jules Dassin, *Illya, Darling*
> Burt Shevelove, *Hallelujah, Baby!*

Composer and Lyricist
> Elmer Bernstein and Carolyn Leigh,
> *How Now, Dow Jones*
> Manos Hadjidakis and Joe Darion,
> *Illya Darling*
> John Kander and Fred Ebb, *The Happy Time*
> * Jule Styne, Betty Comden and Adolph Green, *Hallelujah, Baby!*

Scenic Designer
> Boris Aronson, *The Price*
> * Desmond Heeley, *Rosencrantz and Guildenstern Are Dead*
> Robert Randolph, *Golden Rainbow*
> Peter Wexler, *The Happy Time*

Costume Designer
> Jane Greenwood, *More Stately Mansions*
> * Desmond Heeley, *Rosencrantz and Guildenstern Are Dead*
> Irene Sharaff, *Hallelujah, Baby!*
> Freddy Wittop, *The Happy Time*

Choreographer
> Michael Bennett, *Henry, Sweet Henry*
> Kevin Carlisle, *Hallelujah, Baby!*
> * Gower Champion, *The Happy Time*
> Onna White, *Illya Darling*

Special Awards
> Audrey Hepburn
> Carol Channing
> Pearl Bailey
> David Merrick
> Maurice Chevalier
> APA-Phoenix Theatre
> Marlene Dietrich

1969

Actor (Dramatic)
  Art Carney, *Lovers*
* James Earl Jones, *The Great White Hope*
  Alec McCowen, *Hadrian VII*
  Donald Pleasence, *The Man in the Glass Booth*

Actress (Dramatic)
* Julie Harris, *Forty Carats*
  Estelle Parsons, *Seven Descents of Myrtle*
  Charlotte Rae, *Morning, Noon and Night*
  Brenda Vaccaro, *The Goodbye People*

Actor, Supporting or Featured (Dramatic)
* Al Pacino, *Does a Tiger Wear a Necktie?*
  Richard Castellano, *Lovers and Other Strangers*
  Anthony Roberts, *Play It Again Sam*
  Louis Zorich, *Hadrian VII*

Actress, Supporting or Featured (Dramatic)
* Jane Alexander, *The Great White Hope*
  Diane Keaton, *Play It Again Sam*
  Lauren Jones, *Does a Tiger Wear a Necktie?*
  Anna Manahan, *Lovers*

Actor (Musical)
  Herschel Bernardi, *Zorba*
  Jack Cassidy, *Maggie Flynn*
  Joel Grey, *George M!*
* Jerry Orbach, *Promises, Promises*

Actress (Musical)
  Maria Karnilova, *Zorba*
  * Angela Lansbury, *Dear World*
  Dorothy Loudon, *The Fig Leaves Are Falling*
  Jill O'Hara, *Promises, Promises*

Actor, Supporting or Featured (Musical)
  A. Larry Haines, *Promises, Promises*
  * Ronald Holgate, *1776*
  Edward Winter, *Promises, Promises*

Actress, Supporting or Featured (Musical)
  Sandy Duncan, *Canterbury Tales*
  * Marian Mercer, *Promises, Promises*
  Lorraine Serabian, *Zorba*
  Virginia Vestoff, *1776*

Play
  * *The Great White Hope,* by Howard Sackler, Prod. by Herman Levin
  Hadrian VII, by Peter Luke. Produced by Lester Osterman Productions, Bill Freedman, Charles Kasher
  Lovers by Brian Friel. Produced by Helen Bonfils and Morton Gottlieb
  The Man in the Glass Booth by Robert Shaw. Produced by Glasshouse Productions and Peter Bridge, Ivor David Balding & Associates Ltd. and Edward M. Meyers with Leslie Ogden

Director (Dramatic)
  * Peter Dews, *Hadrian VII*
  Joseph Hardy, *Play It Again Sam*

Harold Pinter, *The Man in the Glass
Booth*
Michael A. Schultz, *Does a Tiger
Wear a Necktie?*

Musical

Hair. Book by Gerome Ragni and
James Rado, music by Galt
MacDermot, lyrics by James Rado.
Produced by Michael Butler.
Promises, Promises. Book by Neil
Simon, music and lyrics by Burt
Bacharach. Produced by David
Merrick
* *1776*. Book by Peter Stone, music
and lyrics by Sherman Edwards.
Produced by Stuart Ostrow.
Zorba. Book by Joseph Stein, music
by John Kander, lyrics by Fred
Ebb. Produced by Harold Prince

Director (Musical)
* Peter Hunt, *1776*
Robert Moore, *Promises, Promises*
Tom O'Horgan, *Hair*
Harold Prince, *Zorba*

Scenic Designer
* Boris Aronson, *Zorba*
Derek Cousins, *Canterbury Tales*
Jo Mielziner, *1776*
Oliver Smith, *Dear World*

Costume Designer
Michael Annals, *Morning, Noon and
Night*
Robert Fletcher, *Hadrian VII*
* Louden Sainthill, *Canterbury Tales*
Patricia Zipprodt, *Zorba*

Choreographer
>Sammy Bayes, *Canterbury Tales*
>Ronald Field, *Zorba*
>* Joe Layton, *George M!*
>Michael Bennett, *Promises, Promises*

Special Awards
>The National Theatre Company of
>Great Britain
>The Negro Ensemble Company
>Rex Harrison
>Leonard Bernstein
>Carol Burnett

The 1970's

"Lighting design as an art and craft in the theatre is one that receives little notice. And rightly so, because light itself is invisible and only enables you to see objects and humans that the light falls upon. For the majority of theatrical productions lighting is an unseen tool that guides the audiences eyes and aids in creating a mood and atmosphere. Thus when lighting is very good it is hardly noticed, and only on a subconscious level can you connect the quality of the lighting with the overall enjoyment and appreciation of the play. Thus for many years I have taken pride in the fact that when I had done my best work no one might notice and thus I could rationalize why I had never received any awards for my work.

Now that I have won a Tony award I must work even harder to make my work unseen and keep it a secret so that more people can enjoy the theatre."

JULES FISHER

1970

Actor (Dramatic)
James Coco, *Last of the Red Hot Lovers*
Frank Grimes, *Borstal Boy*
Stacy Keach, *Indians*
* Fritz Weaver, *Child's Play*

Actress (Dramatic)
Geraldine Brooks, *Brightower*
* Tammy Grimes, *Private Lives* (Revival)
Helen Hayes, *Harvey* (Revival)

Actor, Supporting or Featured (Dramatic)
Joseph Bova, *The Chinese and Dr. Fish*
* Ken Howard, *Child's Play*
Dennis King, *A Patriot for Me*

Actress, Supporting or Featured (Dramatic)
* Blythe Danner, *Butterflies Are Free*
Alice Drummond, *The Chinese and Dr. Fish*
Eileen Heckart, *Butterflies Are Free*
Linda Lavin, *Last of the Red Hot Lovers*

Actor (Musical)
>Len Cariou, *Applause*
>* Cleavon Little, *Purlie*
>Robert Weede, *Cry For Us All*

Actress (Musical)
>* Lauren Bacall, *Applause*
>Katharine Hepburn, *Coco*
>Dilys Watling, *Georgy*

Actor, Supporting or Featured (Musical)
>* René Auberjonois, *Coco*
>Brandon Maggart, *Applause*
>George Rose, *Coco*

Actress, Supporting or Featured (Musical)
>Bonnie Franklin, *Applause*
>Penny Fuller, *Applause*
>Melissa Hart, *Georgy*
>* Melba Moore, *Purlie*

Play
>* *Borstal Boy* by Frank McMahon. Produced by Michael McAloney, Burton C. Kaiser
>*Child's Play* by Robert Marasco. Produced by David Merrick
>*Indians* by Arthur Kopit. Produced by Lyn Austin, Oliver Smith, Joel Schenker, Roger L. Stevens
>*Last of the Red Hot Lovers* by Neil Simon. Produced by Saint-Subber

Director (Dramatic)
>* Joseph Hardy, *Child's Play*
>Milton Katselas, *Butterflies Are Free*
>Tomas MacAnna, *Borstal Boy*
>Robert Moore, *Last of the Red Hot Lovers*

Musical

* *Applause.* Book by Betty Comden and
Adolph Green, music by Charles
Strouse, lyrics by Lee Adams.
Produced by Joseph Kipness and
Lawrence Kasha
Coco. Book and lyrics by Alan Jay
Lerner, music by André
Previn. Produced by Frederick
Brisson
Purlie. Book by Ossie Davis, Philip
Rose, Peter Udell, music by Gary
Geld, lyrics by Peter Udell.
Produced by Philip Rose

Director (Musical)
Michael Benthall, *Coco*
* Ron Field, *Applause*
Philip Rose, *Purlie*

Scenic Designer
Howard Bay, *Cry for Us All*
Ming Cho Lee, *Billy*
* Jo Mielziner, *Child's Play*
Robert Randolph, *Applause*

Costume Designer
Ray Aghayan, *Applause*
* Cecil Beaton, *Coco*
W. Robert Lavine, *Jimmy*
Freddy Wittop, *A Patriot for Me*

Choreographer
Michael Bennett, *Coco*
Grover Dale, *Billy*
* Ron Field, *Applause*
Louis Johnson, *Purlie*

109

Lighting Designer
    * Jo Mielziner, *Child's Play*
    Tharon Musser, *Applause*
    Thomas Skelton, *Indians*

Special Awards
    Noel Coward
    Alfred Lunt and Lynn Fontanne
    New York Shakespeare Festival
    Barbra Streisand

1971

Actor (Dramatic)
    * Brian Bedford, *The School for Wives*
    John Gielgud, *Home*
    Alec McCowen, *The Philanthropist*
    Ralph Richardson, *Home*

Actress (Dramatic)
    Estelle Parsons, *And Miss Reardon Drinks a Little*
    Diana Rigg, *Abelard and Heloise*
    Marian Seldes, *Father's Day*
    * Maureen Stapleton, *Gingerbread Lady*

Actor, Supporting or Featured (Dramatic)
    Ronald Radd, *Abelard and Heloise*
    Donald Pickering, *Conduct Unbecoming*
    * Paul Sand, *Story Theatre*
    Ed Zimmermann, *The Philanthropist*

Actress, Supporting or Featured (Dramatic)
    * Rae Allen, *And Miss Reardon Drinks a Little*

Lili Darvas, *Les Blancs*
Joan Van Ark, *The School for Wives*
Mona Washbourne, *Home*

Actor (Musical)
David Burns, *Lovely Ladies, Kind
    Gentlemen*
Larry Kert, *Company*
* Hal Linden, *The Rothchilds*
Bobby Van, *No, No, Nanette* (Revival)

Actress (Musical)
Susan Browning, *Company*
Sandy Duncan, *The Boy Friend*
* Helen Gallagher, *No, No, Nanette*
Elaine Stritch, *Company*

Actor, Supporting or Featured (Musical)
* Keene Curtis, *The Rothschilds*
Charles Kimbrough, *Company*
Walter Willison, *Two By Two*

Actress, Supporting or Featured (Musical)
Barbara Barrie, *Company*
* Patsy Kelly, *No, No, Nanette*
Pamela Myers, *Company*

Play

Home by David Storey. Produced by
    Alexander H. Cohen
* *Sleuth* by Anthony Shaffer. Produced
    by Helen Bonfils, Morton Gottlieb
    and Michael White
Story Theatre by Paul Sills. Produced
    by Zev Bufman
The Philanthropist by Christopher
    Hampton. Produced by David
    Merrick and Byron Goldman

111

Producer (Dramatic)
    Alexander H. Cohen, *Home*
    David Merrick, *The Philanthropist*
  * Helen Bonfils, Morton Gottlieb and
      Michael White, *Sleuth*
    Zev Bufman, *Story Theatre*

Director (Dramatic)
    Lindsay Anderson, *Home*
  * Peter Brook, *A Midsummer Night's
      Dream*
    Stephen Porter, *The School for Wives*
    Clifford Williams, *Sleuth*

Musical
  * *Company*. Produced by Harold Prince
    The Me Nobody Knows. Produced by J‹
      Britton
    The Rothschilds. Produced by Lester
      Osterman and Hillard Elkins

Producer (Musical)
  * Harold Prince, *Company*
    Jeff Britton, *The Me Nobody Knows*
    Hillard Elkins and Lester Osterman,
      The Rothschilds

Director (Musical)
    Michael Kidd, *The Rothschilds*
    Robert H. Livingston, *The Me Nobody
      Knows*
  * Harold Prince, *Company*
    Burt Shevelove, *No, No, Nanette*

Book (Musical)
  * George Furth, *Company*
    Robert H. Livingston and Herb
      Schapiro, *The Me Nobody Knows*
    Sherman Yellen, *The Rothschilds*

Lyrics (Musical)

Sheldon Harnick, *The Rothschilds*

Will Holt, *The Me Nobody Knows*

  * Stephen Sondheim, *Company*

Score (Musical)

Jerry Bock, *The Rothschilds*

Gary William Friedman, *The Me Nobody Knows*

  * Stephen Sondheim, *Company*

Scenic Designer

  * Boris Aronson, *Company*

John Bury, *The Rothschilds*

Sally Jacobs, *A Midsummer Night's Dream*

Jo Mielziner, *Father's Day*

Costume Designer

  * Raoul Pène Du Bois, *No, No, Nanette*

Jane Greenwood, *Hay Fever* and *Les Blancs*

Freddy Wittop, *Lovely Ladies, Kind Gentlemen*

Choreographer

Michael Bennett, *Company*

Michael Kidd, *The Rothschilds*

  * Donald Saddler, *No, No, Nanette*

Lighting Designer

Robert Ornbo, *Company*

  * H. R. Poindexter, *Story Theatre*

William Ritman, *Sleuth*

Special Awards

Elliot Norton

Ingram Ash

Playbill

Roger L. Stevens

1972

Actor (Dramatic)
> Tom Aldredge, *Sticks and Bones*
> Donald Pleasence, *Wise Child*
> * Cliff Gorman, *Lenny*
> Jason Robards, *The Country Girl*

Actress (Dramatic)
> Eileen Atkins, *Vivat! Vivat Regina!*
> Colleen Dewhurst, *All Over*
> Rosemary Harris, *Old Times*
> * Sada Thompson, *Twigs*

Actor, Supporting or Featured (Dramatic)
> * Vincent Gardenia, *The Prisoner of Second Avenue*
> Douglas Rain, *Vivat! Vivat Regina!*
> Lee Richardson, *Vivat! Vivat Regina!*
> Joe Silver, *Lenny*

Actress, Supporting or Featured (Dramatic)
> Cara Duff-MacCormick, *Moonchildren*
> Mercedes McCambridge, *The Love Suicide at Schofield Barracks*
> Frances Sternhagen, *The Sign in Sidney Brustein's Window* (Revival)
> * Elizabeth Wilson, *Sticks and Bones*

Actor (Musical)
> Clifton Davis, *Two Gentlemen of Verona*
> Barry Bostwick, *Grease*
> Raul Julia, *Two Gentlemen of Verona*
> * Phil Silvers, *A Funny Thing Happened on the Way to the Forum* (Revival)

114

Actress (Musical)

Jonelle Allen, *Two Gentlemen of Verona*

Dorothy Collins, *Follies*

Mildred Natwick, *70 Girls 70*

* Alexis Smith, *Follies*

Actor, Supporting or Featured (Musical)

* Larry Blyden, *A Funny Thing Happened on the Way to the Forum* (Revival)

Timothy Meyers, *Grease*

Gene Nelson, *Follies*

Ben Vereen, *Jesus Christ Superstar*

Actress, Supporting or Featured (Musical)

Adrienne Barbeau, *Grease*

* Linda Hopkins, *Inner City*

Bernadette Peters, *On The Town* (Revival)

Beatrice Wind, *Ain't Supposed to Die a Natural Death*

Play

Old Times by Harold Pinter. Produced by Roger L. Stevens

The Prisoner of Second Avenue by Neil Simon. Produced by Saint-Subber

* *Sticks and Bones* by David Rabe. Produced by New York Shakespeare Festival — Joseph Papp

Vivat! Vivat Regina! by Robert Bolt. Produced by David Merrick and Arthur Cantor

Director (Dramatic)

Jeff Bleckner, *Sticks and Bones*

Gordon Davidson, *The Trial Of The Catonsville Nine*

Peter Hall, *Old Times*
* Mike Nichols, *The Prisoner of
Second Avenue*

Musical

*Ain't Supposed to Die a Natural
Death.* Produced by Eugene
V. Wolsk, Charles Blackwell,
Emanuel Azenberg, Robert
Malina
Follies. Produced by Harold Prince
* *Two Gentlemen of Verona.* Pro-
duced by New York Shakes-
peare Festival — Joseph Papp
Grease. Produced by Kenneth
Waissman and Maxine Fox

Director (Musical)

Gilbert Moses, *Ain't Supposed to
Die a Natural Death*
* Harold Prince and Michael Bennett,
Follies
Mel Shapiro, *Two Gentlemen of
Verona*
Burt Shevelove, *A Funny Thing
Happened on the Way to the
Forum*

Book (Musical)

*Ain't Supposed to Die a Natural
Death,* by Melvin Van Peebles
Follies by James Goldman
Grease by Jim Jacobs and Warren
Casey
* *Two Gentlemen of Verona* by John
Guare and Mel Shapiro

Score

*Ain't Supposed to Die a Natural
Death.* Composer: Melvin Van
Peebles. Lyricist: Melvin Van
Peebles
* *Follies.* Composer: Stephen Sondheim,
Lyricist: Stephen Sondheim.
Jesus Christ Superstar. Composer:
Andrew Lloyd Webber. Lyricist:
Tim Rice
Two Gentlemen of Verona. Composer:
Galt MacDermot. Lyricist: John
Guare

Scenic Designer

* Boris Aronson, *Follies*
John Bury, *Old Times*
Kert Lundell, *Ain't Supposed to
Die a Natural Death*
Robin Wagner, *Jesus Christ Superstar*

Costume Designer

Theoni V. Aldredge, *Two Gentlemen
of Verona*
Randy Barcelo, *Jesus Christ Superstar*
* Florence Klotz, *Follies*
Carrie F. Robbins, *Grease*

Choreographer

* Michael Bennett, *Follies*
Patricia Birch, *Grease*
Jean Erdman, *Two Gentlemen of
Verona*

Lighting Designer

Martin Aronstein, *Ain't Supposed
to Die a Natural Death*
John Bury, *Old Times*
Jules Fisher, *Jesus Christ Superstar*
* Tharon Musser, *Follies*

Special Awards
> The Theatre Guild-American Theatre
> Society
> Richard Rodgers
> *Fiddler on the Roof*
> Ethel Merman

1973

Actor (Dramatic)
> Jack Albertson, *The Sunshine Boys*
> * Alan Bates, *Butley*
> Wilfrid Hyde White, *The Jockey
> Club Stakes*
> Paul Sorvino, *That Championship
> Season*

Actress (Dramatic)
> Jane Alexander, *6 Rms Riv Vu*
> Colleen Dewhurst, *Mourning Becomes
> Electra*
> * Julie Harris, *The Last of Mrs.
> Lincoln*
> Kathleen Widdoes, *Much Ado About
> Nothing*

Actor, Supporting or Featured (Dramatic)
> Barnard Hughes, *Much Ado About
> Nothing*
> * John Lithgow, *The Changing Room*
> John McMartin, *Don Juan*
> Hayward Morse, *Butley*

Actress, Supporting or Featured (Dramatic)
> Maya Angelou, *Look Away*
> * Leora Dana, *The Last of Mrs. Lincoln*
> Katherine Helmond, *The Great God
> Brown*
> Penelope Windust, *Elizabeth I*

Actor (Musical)

    Len Cariou, *A Little Night Music*
    Robert Morse, *Sugar*
    Brock Peters, *Lost in the Stars*
    * Ben Vereen, *Pippin*

Actress (Musical)

    * Glynis Johns, *A Little Night Music*
    Leland Palmer, *Pippin*
    Debbie Reynolds, *Irene* (Revival)
    Marcia Rodd, *Shelter*

Actor, Supporting or Featured (Musical)

    Laurence Guittard, *A Little Night Music*
    * George S. Irving, *Irene*
    Avon Long, *Don't Play Us Cheap*
    Gilbert Price, *Lost in the Stars*

Actress, Supporting or Featured (Musical)

    * Patricia Elliot, *A Little Night Music*
    Hermione Gingold, *A Little Night Music*
    Patsy Kelly, *Irene*
    Irene Ryan, *Pippin*

Play

    Butley by Simon Gray. Produced By Lester Osterman and Richard Horner
    * *That Championship Season* by Jason Miller. Produced by the New York Shakespeare Festival — Joseph Papp
    The Changing Room by David Storey. Produced by Charles Bowden, Lee Reynolds, Isobel Robins
    The Sunshine Boys by Neil Simon. Produced by Emanuel Azenberg and Eugene V. Wolsk

Director (Dramatic)
  * A. J. Antoon, *That Championship
    Season*
  A. J. Antoon, *Much Ado About
    Nothing*
  Alan Arkin, *The Sunshine Boys*
  Michael Rudman, *The Changing Room*

Musical
  * *A Little Night Music.* Produced by
    Harold Prince
  Don't Bother Me, I Can't Cope.
    Produced by Edward Padula
    and Arch Lustberg
  Pippin. Produced by Stuart Ostrow
  Sugar. Produced by David Merrick

Director (Musical)
  Vinnette Carroll, *Don't Bother Me,
    I Can't Cope*
  Gower Champion, *Sugar*
  * Bob Fosse, *Pippin*
  Harold Prince, *A Little Night Music*

Book (Musical)
  * *A Little Night Music* by Hugh
    Wheeler
  Don't Bother Me, I Can't Cope by
    Micki Grant
  Don't Play Us Cheap by Melvin Van
    Peebles
  Pippin by Roger O. Hirson

Score (Musical)
  * *A Little Night Music.* Music and
    lyrics: Stephen Sondheim
  Don't Bother Me, I Can't Cope. Music
    and Lyrics: Micki Grant

Much Ado About Nothing. Music:
Peter Link
Pippin. Music and Lyrics: Stephen
Schwartz

Scenic Designer
Boris Aronson, *A Little Night Music*
David Jenkins, *The Changing Room*
Santo Loquasto, *That Championship
Season*
* Tony Walton, *Pippin*

Costume Designer
Theoni V. Aldredge, *Much Ado About
Nothing*
* Florence Klotz, *A Little Night
Music*
Miles White, *Tricks*
Patricia Zipprodt, *Pippin*

Choreographer
Gower Champion, *Sugar*
* Bob Fosse, *Pippin*
Peter Gennaro, *Irene*
Donald Saddler, *Much Ado About
Nothing*

Lighting Designer
Martin Aronstein, *Much Ado About
Nothing*
Ian Calderon, *That Championship
Season*
* Jules Fisher, *Pippin*
Tharon Musser, *A Little Night Music*

Special Awards
John Lindsay
Actors' Fund of America
Shubert Organization

1974

Actor (Dramatic)
* Michael Moriarty, *Find Your Way Home*
Zero Mostel, *Ulysses in Nighttown*
Jason Robards, *A Moon for the Misbegotten* (Revival)
George C. Scott, *Vanya* (Revival)
Nicol Williamson, *Uncle Vanya*

Actress (Dramatic)
Jane Alexander, *Find Your Way Home*
* Colleen Dewhurst, *A Moon for the Misbegotten*
Julie Harris, *The Au Pair Man*
Madeline Kahn, *Boom Boom Room*
Rachel Roberts, performances with the *New Phoenix Repertory Company*

Actor, Supporting or Featured (Dramatic)
Rene Auberjonois, *The Good Doctor*
* Ed Flanders, *A Moon for the Misbegotten*
Douglas Turner Ward, *The River Niger*
Dick A. Williams, *What the Wine-Sellers Buy*

Actress, Supporting or Featured (Dramatic)
Regina Baff, *Veronica's Room*
Fionnuala Flanagan, *Ulysses in Nighttown*
Charlotte Moore, *Chemin de Fer*
Roxie Roker, *The River Niger*
* Frances Sternhagen, *The Good Doctor*

Actor (Musical)
      Alfred Drake, *Gigi*
      Joe Morton, *Raisin*
    * Christopher Plummer, *Cyrano*
      Lewis J. Stadlen, *Candide*

Actress (Musical)
    * Virginia Capers, *Raisin*
      Carol Channing, *Lorelei*
      Michele Lee, *Seesaw*

Actor, Supporting or Featured (Musical)
      Mark Baker, *Candide*
      Ralph Carter, *Raisin*
    * Tommy Tune, *Seesaw*

Actress, Supporting or Featured (Musical)
      Leigh Berry, *Cyrano*
      Maureen Brennan, *Candide*
      June Gable, *Candide*
      Ernestine Jackson, *Raisin*
    * Janie Sell, *Over Here!*

Play
      Boom Boom Room by David Rabe.
        Produced by Joseph Papp
      The Au Pair Man by Hugh Leonard.
        Produced by Joseph Papp
    * *The River Niger* by Joseph A. Walker.
        Produced by Negro Ensenble Co.,
        Inc.
      Ulysses in Nighttown by Marjorie
        Barkentin. Produced by Alexander
        H. Cohen and Bernard Delfont

Director (Dramatic)
      Burgess Meredith, *Ulysses in*
        Nighttown
      Mike Nichols, *Uncle Vanya*

Stephen Porter, *Chemin de Fer*
* José Quintero, *A Moon for the Misbegotten*
Edwin Sherin, *Find Your Way Home*

Musical

Over Here! Produced by Kenneth Waissman and Maxine Fox
* *Raisin.* Produced by Robert Nemiroff
Seesaw. Produced by Joseph Kipness, Lawrence Kasha, James Nederlander, George M. Steinbrenner III, Lorin E. Price

Director (Musical)

Michael Bennett, *Seesaw*
Donald McKayle, *Raisin*
* Harold Prince, *Candide*
Tom Moore, *Over Here!*

Book (Musical)

* *Candide* by Hugh Wheeler
Raisin by Robert Nemiroff and Charlotte Zaltzberg
Seesaw by Michael Bennett

Score

* *Gigi.* Music: Frederick Loewe. Lyrics: Alan Jay Lerner
The Good Doctor. Music: Peter Link. Lyrics: Neil Simon
Raisin. Music: Judd Woldin. Lyrics: Robert Brittan
Seesaw. Music: Cy Coleman. Lyrics: Dorothy Fields

Scenic Designer

John Conklin, *The Au Pair Man*
* Franne and Eugene Lee, *Candide*

124

Santo Loquasto, *What the Wine-*
Sellers Buy
Oliver Smith, *Gigi*
Ed Wittstein, *Ulysses in Nighttown*

Costume Designer
Theoni V. Aldredge, *The Au Pair Man*
Finlay James, *Crown Matrimonial*
* Franne Lee, *Candide*
Oliver Messel, *Gigi*
Carrie F. Robbins, *Over Here!*

Choreographer
* Michael Bennett, *Seesaw*
Patricia Birch, *Over Here!*
Donald McKayle, *Raisin*

Lighting Designer
Martin Aronstein, *Boom Boom Room*
Ken Billington, *The Visit* (Revival)
Ben Edwards, *A Moon for the*
Misbegotten
* Jules Fisher, *Ulysses in Nighttown*
Tharon Musser, *The Good Doctor*

Special Awards
Liza Minnelli
Bette Midler
Peter Cook and Dudley Moore,
Good Evening
A Moon for the Misbegotten
Candide
Actors' Equity Association
Theatre Development Fund
John F. Wharton
Harold Friedlander

125

1975

Actor (Dramatic)
    James Dale, *Scapino*
    Peter Firth, *Equus*
    Henry Fonda, *Clarence Darrow*
    Ben Gazarra, *Hughie and Duet*
* John Kani and Winston
      Ntshona, *Sizwe Banzi is Dead*
      and The Island
    John Wood, *Sherlock Holmes*

Actress (Dramatic)
    Elizabeth Ashley, *Cat on a Hot Tin Roof*
* Ellen Burstyn, *Same Time, Next Year*
    Diana Rigg, *The Misanthrope*
    Maggie Smith, *Private Lives*
    Liv Ullmann, *A Doll's House*

Actor, Supporting or Featured (Dramatic)
    Larry Blyden, *Absurd Person Singular*
    Leonard Frey, *The National Health*
* Frank Langella, *Seascape*
    Philip Locke, *Sherlock Holmes*
    George Rose, *My Fat Friend*
    Dick Anthony Williams, *Black Picture Show*

Actress, Supporting or Featured (Dramatic)
    Linda Miller, *Black Picture Show*
* Rita Moreno, *The Ritz*
    Geraldine Page, *Absurd Person Singular*
    Carole Shelley, *Absurd Person Singular*
    Elizabeth Spriggs, *London Assurance*
    Frances Sternhagen, *Equus*

Actor (Musical)
* John Cullum, *Shenandoah*
  Joel Grey, *Goodtime Charley*
  Raul Julia, *Where's Charley?*
  Eddie Mekka, *The Lieutenant*
  Robert Preston, *Mack and Mabel*

Actress (Musical)
  Lola Falana, *Doctor Jazz*
* Angela Lansbury, *Gypsy*
  Bernadette Peters, *Mack and Mabel*
  Ann Reinking, *Goodtime Charley*

Actor, Supporting or Featured (Musical)
  Tom Aldredge, *Where's Charley?*
  John Bottoms, *Dance with Me*
  Douglas Henning, *The Magic Show*
  Gilbert Price, *The Night That Made
     America Famous*
* Ted Ross, *The Wiz*
  Richard B. Shull, *Goodtime Charley*

Actress, Supporting or Featured (Musical)
* Dee Dee Bridgewater, *The Wiz*
  Susan Browning, *Goodtime Charley*
  Zan Charisse, *Gypsy*
  Taina Elg, *Where's Charley?*
  Kelly Garrett, *The Night That Made
     America Famous*
  Donna Theodore, *Shenandoah*

Play

* *Equus* by Peter Shaffer. Produced by
     Kermit Bloomgarden and Doris
     Cole Abrahams
  Same Time, Next Year by Bernard
     Slade. Produced by Morton
     Gottlieb

127

Seascape by Edward Albee. Produced
   by Richard Barr, Charles
   Woodward and Clinton Wilder
Short Eyes by Miguel Pinero. Pro-
   duced by Joseph Papp, New York
   Shakespeare Festival
Sizwe Banzi is Dead and The Island by
   Athol Fugard, John Kani and
   Winston Ntshona. Produced by
   Hillard Elkins, Lester Osterman
   Productions, Bernard Delfont
   and Michael White
The National Health by Peter
   Nichols. Produced by Circle in
   the Square, Inc.

Director (Dramatic)
   Arvin Brown, *The National Health*
 * John Dexter, *Equus*
   Frank Dunlop, *Scapino*
   Ronald Eyre, *London Assurance*
   Athol Fugard, *Sizwe Banzi is Dead
      and The Island*
   Gene Saks, *Same Time, Next Year*

Musical

   Mack and Mabel. Produced by David
      Merrick
   The Lieutenant. Produced by Joseph
      Kutrzeba and Spofford Beadle
   Shenandoah. Produced by Philip
      Rose, Gloria and Louis K. Sher
 * *The Wiz*. Produced by Ken Harper

Director (Musical)
   Gower Champion, *Mack and Mabel*
   Grover Dale, *The Magic Show*
 * Geoffrey Holder, *The Wiz*
   Arthur Laurents, *Gypsy*

128

Book (Musical)

Mack and Mabel by Michael Stewart
* Shenandoah by James Lee Barrett,
Peter Udell and Philip Rose
The Lieutenant by Gene Curty,
Nitra Scharfman, Chuck Strand
The Wiz by William F. Brown

Score

Letter for Queen Victoria. Music:
Alan Lloyd. Lyrics: Alan Lloyd
Shenandoah. Music: Gary Geld.
Lyrics: Peter Udell
The Lieutenant. Music: Gene Curty,
Nitra Scharfman, Chuck Strand.
Lyrics: Gene Curty, Nitra Scharf-
man, Chuck Strand
* The Wiz. Music: Charlie Smalls.
Lyrics: Charlie Smalls

Scenic Designer

Scott Johnson, Dance With Me
Tanya Moiseiwitsch, The Misan-
thrope
William Ritman, God's Favorite
Rouben Ter-Arutunian, Goodtime
Charley
* Carl Toms, Sherlock Holmes
Robert Wagner, Mack and Mabel

Costume Designer

Arthur Boccia, Where's Charley?
Raoul Pene du Bois, Doctor Jazz
* Geoffrey Holder, The Wiz
Willa Kim, Goodtime Charley
Tanya Moiseiwitsch, The Misan-
thrope
Patricia Zipprodt, Mack and Mabel

129

Choreographer

Gower Champion, *Mack and Mabel*
* George Faison, *The Wiz*
Donald McKayle, *Doctor Jazz*
Margo Sappington, *Where's Charley?*
Robert Tucker, *Shenandoah*
Joel Zwick, *Dance with Me*

Lighting Designer

Chip Monk, *The Rocky Horror Show*
Abe Feder, *Goodtime Charley*
* Neil Peter Jampolis, *Sherlock Holmes*
Andy Phillips, *Equus*
Thomas Skelton, *All God's Chillun*
James Tilton, *Seascape*

Special Awards

Neil Simon
Al Hirschfeld

1976

Actor (Play)

Moses Gunn, *The Poison Tree*
George C. Scott, *Death of a Salesman*
Donald Sinden, *Habeas Corpus*
* John Wood, *Travesties*

Actress (Play)

Tovah Feldshuh, *Yentl*
Rosemary Harris, *The Royal Family*
Lynn Redgrave, *Mrs. Warren's Profession*
* Irene Worth, *Sweet Bird of Youth*

Actor (Featured role - Play)
    Barry Bostwick, *They Knew What*
    They Wanted
    Gabriel Dell, *Lamppost Reunion*
  * Edward Herrmann, *Mrs. Warren's*
    Profession
    Daniel Seltzer, *Knock Knock*

Actress (Featured role - Play)
    Marybeth Hurt, *Trelawny of the*
    'Wells'
  * Shirley Knight, *Kennedy's Children*
    Lois Nettleton, *They Knew What*
    They Wanted
    Meryl Streep, *27 Wagons Full of*
    Cotton

Actor (Musical)
    Mako, *Pacific Overtures*
    Jerry Orbach, *Chicago*
    Ian Richardson, *My Fair Lady*
  * George Rose, *My Fair Lady*

Actress (Musical)
  * Donna McKechnie, *A Chorus Line*
    Vivian Reed, *Bubbling Brown Sugar*
    Chita Rivera, *Chicago*
    Gwen Verdon, *Chicago*

Actor (Featured role - Musical)
    Robert LuPone, *A Chorus Line*
    Charles Repole, *Very Good Eddie*
    Isao Sato, *Pacific Overtures*
  * Sammy Williams, *A Chorus Line*

Actress (Featured role - Musical)
  * Carole Bishop, *A Chorus Line*
    Priscilla Lopez, *A Chorus Line*

Patti LuPone, *The Robber Bride-groom*
Virginia Seidel, *Very Good Eddie*

Play

The First Breeze of Summer by Leslie Lee. Produced by Negro Ensemble Co., Inc.

Knock Knock by Jules Feiffer. Produced by Harry Rigby and Terry Allen Kramer

Lamppost Reunion by Louis LaRusso II. Produced by Joe Garofalo

* *Travesties* by Tom Stoppard. Produced by David Merrick, Doris Cole Abrahams and Burry Fredrik in association with S. Spencer Davids and Eddie Kulukundis

Director (Play)

Arvin Brown, *Ah Wilderness*
Marshall W. Mason, *Knock Knock*
* Ellis Rabb, *The Royal Family*
Peter Wood, *Travesties*

Musical

* *A Chorus Line.* Produced by Joseph Papp, NY Shakespeare Festival

Bubbling Brown Sugar. Produced by J. Lloyd Grant, Richard Bell, Robert M. Cooper and Ashton Springer in association with Moe Septee, Inc.

Chicago. Produced by Robert Fryer and James Cresson

Pacific Overtures. Produced by Harold Prince in association with Ruth Mitchell

Director (Musical)
* Michael Bennet, *A Chorus Line*
  Bob Fosse, *Chicago*
  Bill Gile, *Very Good Eddie*
  Harold Prince, *Pacific Overtures*

Book (Musical)
* *A Chorus Line* by James Kirkwood
  and Nicholas Dante
  Chicago by Fred Ebb and Bob Fosse
  Pacific Overtures by John Weidman
  The Robber Bridegroom by Alfred
  Uhry

Score
* *A Chorus Line.* Music: Marvin
  Hamlisch. Lyrics: Edward Kleban
  Chicago. Music: John Kander.
  Lyrics: Fred Ebb
  Pacific Overtures. Music: Stephen
  Sondheim. Lyrics: Stephen
  Sondheim
  Treemonisha. Music: Scott Joplin.
  Lyrics: Scott Joplin

Scenic Designers
* Boris Aronson, *Pacific Overtures*
  Ben Edwards, *A Matter of Gravity*
  David Mitchell, *Trelawny of the
  'Wells'*
  Tony Walton, *Chicago*

Costume Designers
  Theoni V. Aldredge, *A Chorus Line*
* Florence Klotz, *Pacific Overtures*
  Ann Roth, *The Royal Family*
  Patricia Zipprodt, *Chicago*

133

Lighting Designer
>Ian Calderon, *Trelawny of the 'Wells'*
>Jules Fisher, *Chicago*
>* Tharon Musser, *A Chorus Line*
>Tharon Musser, *Pacific Overtures*

Choreographer
>* Michael Bennet and Bob Avian, *A Chorus Line*
>Patricia Birch, *Pacific Overtures*
>Bob Fosse, *Chicago*
>Billy Wilson, *Bubbling Brown Sugar*

Special Awards
>Mathilde Pincus, *Circle in the Square*
>Thomas H. Fitzgerald, *The Arena Stage*

1977

Actor (Play)
>Tom Courtenay, *Otherwise Engaged*
>Ben Gazzara, *Who's Afraid of Virginia Woolf?*
>* Al Pacino, *The Basic Training of Pavlo Hummel*
>Ralph Richardson, *No Man's Land*

Actress (Play)
>Colleen Dewhurst, *Who's Afraid of Virginia Woolf?*
>* Julie Harris, *The Belle of Amherst*

Liv Ullmann, *Anna Christie*
Irene Worth, *The Cherry Orchard*

Actor (Featured Role - Play)
Bob Dishy, *Sly Fox*
Joe Fields, *The Basic Training of
Pavlo Hummel*
Laurence Luckinbill, *The Shadow
Box*
* Jonathan Pryce, *Comedians*

Actress (Featured Role - Play)
* Trazana Beverley, *For Colored Girls
Who Have Considered Suicide/
When The Rainbow is Enuf*
Patricia Elliott, *The Shadow Box*
Rose Gregorio, *The Shadow Box*
Mary McCarty, *Anna Christie*

Actor (Musical)
* Barry Bostwick, *The Robber Bride-
groom*
Robert Guillaume, *Guys and Dolls*
Raul Julia, *Threepenny Opera*
Reid Shelton, *Annie*

Actress (Musical)
Clamma Dale, *Porgy and Bess*
Ernestine Jackson, *Guys and Dolls*
* Dorothy Loudon, *Annie*
Andrea McArdle, *Annie*

Actor (Featured Role - Musical)
* Lenny Baker, *I Love My Wife*
David Kernan, *Side By Side By
Sondheim*
Larry Marshall, *Porgy and Bess*

135

Ned Sherrin, *Side By Side By Sondheim*

Actress (Featured Role - Musical)

Ellen Green, *Threepenny Opera*

* Delores Hall, *Your Arm's Too Short To Box With God*

Millicent Martin, *Side By Side By Sondheim*

Julie N. McKenzie, *Side By Side By Sondheim*

Play

For Colored Girls who have Considered Suicide/When the Rainbow is Enuf by Ntozake Shange. Produced by Joseph Papp

Otherwise Engaged by Simon Gray. Produced by Michael Codron, Frank Milton and James M. Nederlanger

Streamers by David Rabe. Produced by Joseph Papp

* *The Shadow Box* by Michael Cristofer. Produced by Allan Francis, Ken Marsolais, Lester Osterman, and Leonard Soloway

Director (Play)

* Gordon Davidson, *The Shadow Box*

Ulu Grosbard, *American Buffalo*

Mike Nichols, *Comedians*

Mike Nichols, *Streamers*

Musical

* *Annie*. Produced by Lewis Allen, Mike Nichols, Irwin Meyer and Stephen R. Friedman

Happy End. Produced by Michael Harvey
and The Chelsea Theatre Center
I Love My Wife. Produced by Terry Allen
Kramer and Harry Rigby in associa-
tion with Joseph Kipness
Side by Side By Sondheim. Produced by
Harold Prince in association with
Ruth Mitchell

Director (Musical)
Vinnette Carroll, *Your Arm's Too Short
To Box With God*
Martin Charnin, *Annie*
Jack O'Brien, *Porgy and Bess*
* Gene Saks, *I Love My Wife*

Book (Musical)
* *Annie* by Thomas Meehan
Happy End by Elisabeth Hauptmann.
Adaptation by Michael Feingold
I Love My Wife by Michael Stewart
Your Arm's Too Short To Box With God by
Vinnette Carroll

Score
* *Annie.* Music: Charles Strouse.
Lyrics: Martin Charnin
Godspell. Music: Stephen Schwartz.
Lyrics: Bertolt Brecht. Lyrics
Adapted by: Michael Feingold
I Love My Wife. Music: Cy Coleman.
Lyrics: Michael Stewart

Scenic Designer
Santo Loquasto, *American Buffalo*
Santo Loquasto, *Threepenny Opera*
* David Mitchell, *Annie*
Robert Randolph, *Porgy and Bess*

Costume Designer
* Theoni V. Aldredge, *Annie*
  Theoni V. Aldredge, *Threepenny Opera*
* Santo Loquasto, *The Cherry Orchard*
  Nancy Potts, *Porgy and Bess*

Lighting Designer
  John Bury, *No Man's Land*
  Pat Collins, *Threepenny Opera*
  Neil Peter Jampolis, *The Innocents*
* Jennifer Tipton, *The Cherry Orchard*

Choreographer
  Talley Beatty, *Your Arm's Too Short To
  Box With God*
  Patricia Birch, *Music Is*
* Peter Gennaro, *Annie*
  Onna White, *I Love My Wife*

Most Innovative Production of a Revival
  Guys and Dolls. Produced by Moe Septee
  in association with Victor H.
  Potamkin, Carmen F. Zollo and
  Ashton Springer.
* *Porgy and Bess.* Produced by Sherwin M.
  Goldman and Houston Grand Opera
  The Cherry Orchard. Produced by Joseph
  Papp
  Threepenny Opera. Produced by Joseph
  Papp

Special Awards
  Lily Tomlin
  Barry Manilow
  Diana Ross
  National Theatre For The Deaf
  Mark Taper Forum
  Equity Library Theatre

138

1978

Actor (Play)

       Hume Cronyn, *The Gin Game*

* Barnard Hughes, *Da*

       Frank Langella, *Dracula*

       Jason Robards, *A Touch of the Poet*

Actress (Play)

       Anne Bancroft, *Golda*

       Anita Gillette, *Chapter Two*

       Estelle Parsons, *Miss Margarida's Way*

* Jessica Tandy, *The Gin Game*

Actor (Featured Role - Play)

       Morgan Freeman, *The Mighty Gents*

       Victor Garber, *Deathtrap*

       Cliff Gorman, *Chapter Two*

* Lester Rawlins, *Da*

Actress (Featured Role - Play)

       Starletta DuPois, *The Mighty Gents*

       Swoosie Kurtz, *Tartuffe*

       Marian Seldes, *Deathtrap*

* Ann Wedgeworth, *Chapter Two*

Actor (Musical)

       Eddie Bracken, *Hello, Dolly!*

* John Cullum, *On The Twentieth
        Century*

       Barry Nelson, *The Act*

       Gilbert Price, *Timbuktu!*

Actress (Musical)

Madeline Kahn, *On The Twentieth Century*

Eartha Kitt, *Timbuktu!*

* Liza Minelli, *The Act*

Frances Sternhagen, *Angel*

Actor (Featured Role - Musical)

Steven Boockvor, *Working*

Wayne Cilento, *Dancin'*

Rex Everhart, *Working*

* Kevin Kline, *On The Twentieth Century*

Actress (Featured Role - Musical)

* Nell Carter, *Ain't Misbehavin'*

Imogene Coca, *On The Twentieth Century*

Ann Reinking, *Dancin'*

Charlaine Woodard, *Ain't Misbehavin'*

Play

Chapter Two by Neil Simon. Produced by Emanuel Azenberg

* *Da* by Hugh Leonard. Produced by Lester Osterman, Marilyn Strauss and Marc Howard

Deathtrap by Ira Levin. Produced by Alfred De Liagre, Jr. and Roger L. Stevens

The Gin Game by D. L. Coburn. Produced by The Shubert Organization, Hume Cronyn and Mike Nichols

Director (Play)

* Melvin Bernhardt, *Da*

Robert Moore, *Deathtrap*

Mike Nichols, *The Gin Game*

Dennis Rosa, *Dracula*

140

Musical
  * *Ain't Misbehavin'*. Produced by Emanuel
    Azenberg, Dasha Epstein, The
    Shubert Organization, Jane Gaynor
    and Ron Dante
    Dancin'. Produced by Jules Fisher, The
    Shubert Organization and Columbia
    Pictures
    On The Twentieth Century. Produced by
    The Producers Circle 2, Inc. (Robert
    Fryer, Mary Lea Johnson, James
    Cresson, Martin Richards), Joseph
    Harris, and Ira Bernstein
    Runaways. Produced by Joseph Papp

Director (Musical)
    Bob Fosse, *Dancin'*
  * Richard Maltby, Jr., *Ain't Misbehavin'*
    Harold Prince, *On The Twentieth
    Century*
    Elizabeth Swados, *Runaways*

Book (Musical)
    A History of the American Film by
    Christopher Durang
  * *On The Twentieth Century* by Betty
    Comden and Adolph Green
    Runaways by Elizabeth Swados
    Working by Stephen Schwartz

Score
    The Act. Music: John Kander. Lyrics:
    Fred Ebb
  * *On The Twentieth Century*. Music: Cy
    Coleman. Lyrics: Betty Comden and
    Adolph Green
    Runaways. Music: Elizabeth Swados.
    Lyrics: Elizabeth Swados

141

Working. Music: Craig Carnelia, Micki Grant, Mary Rodgers/Susan Birkenhead, Stephen Schwartz and James Taylor. Lyrics: Craig Carnelia, Micki Grant, Mary Rodgers/Susan Birkenhead, Stephen Schwartz and James Taylor

Scenic Designer
 Zack Brown, *The Importance of Being Ernest*
 Edward Gorey, *Dracula*
 David Mitchell, *Working*
 * Robin Wagner, *On The Twentieth Century*

Costume Designer
 * Edward Gorey, *Dracula*
 Halston, *The Act*
 Geoffrey Holder, *Timbuktu!*
 Willa Kim, *Dancin'*

Lighting Designer
 Jules Fisher, *Beatlemania*
 * Jules Fisher, *Dancin'*
 Tharon Musser, *The Act*
 Ken Billington, *Working*

Choreographer
 Arthur Faria, *Ain't Misbehavin'*
 * Bob Fosse, *Dancin'*
 Ron Lewis, *The Act*
 Elizabeth Swados, *Runaways*

Most Innovative Production of a Revival
 * *Dracula.* Produced by Jujamcyn Theatre, Elizabeth I. McCann, John Wulp, Victor Lurie, Nelle Nugent, Max Weitzenhoffer

142

Tartuffe. Produced by Circle in the
Square
Timbuktu! Produced by Luther Davis
A Touch of the Poet. Produced by Elliot
Martin

Special Award
The Long Wharf Theatre

1979

Actor (Play)
Philip Anglim, *The Elephant Man*
* Tom Conti, *Whose Life Is It Anyway?*
Jack Lemmon, *Tribute*
Alec McCowen, *St. Mark's Gospel*

Actress (Play)
Jane Alexander, *First Monday In October*
* Constance Cummings, *Wings*
* Carole Shelley, *The Elephant Man*
Frances Sternhagen, *On Golden Pond*

Actor (Featured Role - Play)
Bob Balaban, *The Inspector General*
* Michael Gough, *Bedroom Farce*
Joseph Maher, *Spokesong*
Edward James Olmos, *Zoot Suit*

Actress (Featured Role - Play)
* Joan Hickson, *Bedroom Farce*
Laurie Kennedy, *Man And Superman*
Susan Littler, *Bedroom Farce*
Mary-Joan Negro, *Wings*

Actor (Musical)
* * Len Cariou, *Sweeney Todd*
* Vincent Gardenia, *Ballroom*
* Joel Grey, *The Grand Tour*
* Robert Klein, *They're Playing Our Song*

Actress (Musical)
* Tovah Feldshuh, *Sarava*
* * Angela Lansbury, *Sweeney Todd*
* Dorothy Loudon, *Ballroom*
* Alexis Smith, *Platinum*

Actor (Featured Role - Musical)
* Richard Cox, *Platinum*
* * Henderson Forsythe, *The Best Little Whorehouse in Texas*
* Gregory Hines, *Eubie!*
* Ron Holgate, *The Grand Tour*

Actress (Featured Role - Musical)
* Joan Ellis, *The Best Little Whorehouse in Texas*
* * Carlin Glynn, *The Best Little Whorehouse In Texas*
* Millicent Martin, *King Of Hearts*
* Maxine Sullivan, *My Old Friends*

Play

Bedroom Farce by Alan Ayckbourn. Produced by Robert Whitehead, Roger L. Stevens, George W. George and Frank Milton

* *The Elephant Man* by Bernard Pomerance. Produced by Richmond Crinkley, Elizabeth I. McCann and Nelle Nugent

Whose Life Is It Anyway? by Brian Clark. Produced by Emanuel Azenberg, James Nederlander and Ray Cooney

144

Wings by Arthur Kopit. Produced by The
Kennedy Center

Director (Play)
Alan Ayckbourn and Peter Hall,
Bedroom Farce
Paul Giovanni, *The Crucifer of Blood*
* Jack Hofsiss, *The Elephant Man*
Michael Lindsay-Hogg, *Whose Life Is It
Anyway?*

Musical
Ballroom. Produced by Michael Bennett,
Bob Avian, Bernard Gersten and
Susan MacNair
* *Sweeney Todd.* Produced by Richard
Barr, Charles Woodward, Robert
Fryer, Mary Lea Johnson and Martin
Richards
The Best Little Whorehouse in Texas.
Produced by Universal Pictures
They're Playing our Song. Produced by
Emanuel Azenberg

Director (Musical)
Michael Bennett, *Ballroom*
Peter Masterson and Tommy Tune, *The
Best Little Whorehouse In Texas*
Robert Moore, *They're Playing Our Song*
* Harold Prince, *Sweeney Todd*

Book (Musical)
Ballroom by Jerome Kass
* *Sweeney Todd* by Hugh Wheeler
The Best Little Whorehouse in Texas by
Larry L. King and Peter Masterson
They're Playing our Song by Neil Simon

145

Score

Carmelina. Music: Burton Lane. Lyrics: Alan Jay Lerner

Eubie! Music: Eubie Blake. Lyrics: Noble Sissle, Andy Razaf, F. E. Miller, Johnny Brandon and Jim Europe

* *Sweeney Todd.* Music: Stephen Sondheim. Lyrics: Stephen Sondheim

The Grand Tour. Music: Jerry Herman. Lyrics: Jerry Herman

Scenic Designer

Karl Eigsti, *Knockout*

David Jenkins, *The Elephant Man*

* Eugene Lee, *Sweeney Todd*

John Wulp, *The Crucifer of Blood*

Costume Designer

Theoni V. Aldredge, *Ballroom*

* Franne Lee, *Sweeney Todd*

Ann Roth, *The Crucifer of Blood*

Julie Weiss, *The Elephant Man*

Lighting Designer

Ken Billington, *Sweeney Todd*

Beverly Emmons, *The Elephant Man*

* Roger Morgan, *The Crucifer of Blood*

Tharon Musser, *Ballroom*

Choreographer

* Michael Bennett and Bob Avian, *Ballroom*

Henry LeTang and Billy Wilson, Eubie!

Dan Siretta, *Whoopee!*

Tommy Tune, *The Best Little Whorehouse in Texas*

146

Special Awards
Henry Fonda
Walter F. Diehl
Eugene O'Neill Memorial Theatre
  Center
American Conservatory Theater

Tony Awards Regulations*

ADMINISTRATION

The Tony Awards Administration Committee of The League of New York Theatres and Producers, Inc., shall administer the Tony Awards subject to the authority of the Board of Governors. All decisions of the Tony Awards Administration Committee concerning eligibility for the Awards and all other matters relating to their administration and presentation shall, subject to the authority of the Board of Governors, be final. The Tony Awards Administration Committee shall consist of seven persons appointed by The League of New York Theatres and Producers, Inc. and three persons appointed by the American Theatre Wing.

ELIGIBILITY

Theatres

Legitimate theatrical productions opening in an eligible Broadway theatre (a list of eligible theatres is attached), between the Eligibility Date of the prior year and the Eligibility Date of the current year, shall be eligible in various categories for nomination for a Tony® Award. If a nominated production has not officially opened in an eligible Broadway theatre on or before the date on which the Tony Administration Committee shall have

---

*The following rules with respect to the Tony® Awards are for the 1978–80 season; they are for information only and subject to change without notice.

established as a cut-off date, said production shall lose its eligibility to receive an award in any category and shall be removed from the ballot. This production will then be eligible for consideration in the following Tony Award season. The date on which the ballots are to be sent shall be no later than fourteen (14) days prior to the date on which the awards are to be presented. Revivals shall be eligible in those categories in which the elements of the productions do not, in the judgement of the Tony Awards Administration Committee, substantially duplicate a prior Broadway production of the play.

Eligibility for Nomination

There shall be established an Eligibility Committee, the purposes of which shall be to recommend a list of the possible nominees in each Award category and to recommend whether a sufficient number of possible nominees exist in quality or quantity to merit the granting of an Award in the applicable category for the current year. The recommendations of the Eligibility Committee shall be made to the Tony Awards Administration Committee, which shall make the final decision. The determinations of the Eligibility Committee shall be based on the opening night program together with any additional guidelines promulgated by the Tony Awards Administration Committee.

The list of possible nominees shall be submitted to the Nominating Committee within 24 hours following the last scheduled opening prior to the Eligibility Date of the current year. The determinations of the Nominating Committee must be based on the list and ballot so submitted and such ballot must be returned in a sealed envelope by messenger (to be supplied by the League) to the independent accounting firm selected pursuant to these Regulations by the close of the business on the next business day following the Eligibility Date.

The Eligibility Committee shall consist of three persons designated by the Tony Awards Administration Committee. Said persons shall not be members of either the League of New York Theatres and Producers, Inc. or the American Theatre Wing. Nor can said persons serve on both the Eligibility Committee and the Nominating Committee. Said persons shall have theatrically recognized backgrounds, shall reside in or about New York City and shall have access to tickets to all eligible productions.

The Eligibility Committee shall meet as required during the Eligibility Year in order to review and update the eligibility list.

THE AWARDS PRESENTATION AND ELIGIBILITY DATE

The Awards shall be presented during the theatrical season but not earlier than January 1st of such season. The date of the presentation ceremony shall be announced as soon as it has been determined.

The Eligibility Date for nominations shall be announced as soon as it has been determined

CATEGORIES OF AWARDS

The Awards may, subject to eligibility for nomination, be made in the following categories:

Play—*Award to Author; Award to Producer*
Musical—*Award to Producer*
Book of a Musical
Score (*Music and Lyrics*)
Performance by an Actor in a Play
Performance by an Actress in a Play
Performance by an Actor in a Musical
Performance by an Actress in a Musical
Performance by a Featured Actor in a Play
Performance by a Featured Actress in a Play
Performance by a Featured Actor in a Musical
Performance by a Featured Actress in a Musical
Direction of a Play
Direction of a Musical
Scenic Design
Costume Design
Lighting Design
Choreography

Special Tony Awards may be given at the discretion of the Tony Awards Administration Committee.

151

SELECTION OF WINNERS OF REGULAR AWARDS

The Nominating Committee

The Nominating Committee shall be appointed by the Tony Awards Administration Committee and shall consist of from five (5) to fourteen (14) persons. The Nominating Committee shall be selected so as to assure that each eligible production and performer shall have been seen by as many members as possible. At no time shall the Nominating Committee be required to meet.

Each member of the Nominating Committee shall receive a ballot and a list of possible nominees from the Eligibility Committee within 24 hours following the last scheduled opening prior to the Eligibility Date of the current year. The vote of each member of the Nominating Committee must be based on the ballot and list so submitted. The ballot of each member of the Nominating Committee must be returned to the independent accounting firm selected pursuant to these Regulations by the close of business on the next business day following the Eligibility Date. The independent accounting firm shall tabulate the votes of the Nominating committee and shall announce the results to the Tony Awards Administration Committee.

The voting for nominees shall be on a cumulative or weighted basis. Each category must receive four votes on a cumulative or weighted basis. For example, if there are twenty possible nominees in a category, the vote shall be 4-3-2-1 in a descending order of preference of the member of the Nominating Committee. The weight given will depend upon the discretion of the person voting. The vote of a member of the Nominating Committee will be invalid unless four votes have been cast in each category in the manner described above.

The Number of Nominees

There shall be four nominees in each category. The nominations shall be conferred upon those eligible persons or productions in each category that receive the four highest total votes based on the cumulative or weighted system described above. In the event the vote of the Nominating Committee results in a tie that would otherwise necessitate more than four nominations in a category, said tie shall be broken in the following manner. The independent accounting firm shall determine which person or production among those tied received the highest number of "4" votes. The person or production with the highest number of "4" votes among those tied shall receive the nomination. If any of those tied have the same number of "4" votes, the independent accounting firm shall then determine which of said persons or productions received the highest number of "3" votes, in which event the person or production with the highest number of "3" votes shall receive the nomination. Should further ties still result, the independent accounting firm shall continue the process to determine which of the possible nominees among those tied received the highest number of "2" votes, in which event the nomination shall be conferred upon the person or production with the highest number of "2" votes.

Persons Eligible to Vote for Winners

The persons eligible to vote for the winners of the Tony Awards shall be the members of the governing boards of the following organizations:

1. Actors' Equity Association
2. The Dramatists Guild
3. Society of Stage Directors and Choreographers
4. United Scenic Artists and

those persons whose names appear on the First and Second Night Press lists, the membership of The League of New York Theatres and Producers, Inc., and the Board of Directors of the American Theatre Wing.

The Tony Administration Committee shall have the right, at its discretion, to remove any person from eligibility to vote in the current year in the event said person has not exercised his/her right to vote in the prior year.

Ballots of Persons Eligible to Vote for Winners

No ballot shall be counted unless the voter casting it has certified to the League that with respect to each category in which he has voted, he has seen a performance of each production which has been nominated for an Award and a performance by each nominated performer in the production for which he has been nominated. The ballot may provide that marking and returning it constitutes such a certificate.

Attendance at Nominated Productions

Producers of those productions which are nominated for Awards or with which any individual nominee is associated may invite eligible voters to attend performances of their productions, and a list of all such eligible voters shall be promptly sent to each such producer.

Independent Accounting Firm

An independent accounting firm shall be jointly selected by the Tony Awards Administration Committee, the producers of the Tony Awards television program and the television network over which the program is broadcast. The firm selected shall mail a ballot containing the names of the nominees to each eligible voter, with a request to mail completed ballots directly to the independent accounting firm. Such firm shall count and tabulate the ballots and certify the winners to the League.

Selection of Winners

The winner in each category shall be the nominee in that category receiving the highest number of votes. No tabulation of the numbers of votes for each nominee shall be made public, and the names of the winners shall not be made public until the presentation of the Awards.

USE OF TONY AWARDS DESIGNATION IN ADVERTISING

Whenever the Tony Award designation is used in advertising media by or on behalf of a nominee or winner, such use must conform to the following conditions:

In the case of a nominee:

Such use must specify the category for which the nomination is made as well as the fact that the nominee has received a nomination, not an Award.

To accomplish these objectives, use of the words "Tony Award" must immediately precede or follow the words "Nominated for", "Nominee" or "nomination" in the same size type as the words "Tony Awards".

Once the Awards have been announced for any given year, the use of the Tony Award designation on behalf of a nominee in any advertising media in the metropolitan New York area shall be discontinued within three months following the date of said announcement.

In the case of a winner:

Such use must specify the year and the category for which the Award was granted and such specification must immediately precede or follow the words "Tony Award" in the same size type as the words "Tony Award."

If, in the sole opinion of the Tony Awards Administration Committee, any of the above provisions have been violated, said violation must be corrected within three days following the delivery of written notice of such violation. If, in the case of a nominee, such violation has not been so corrected within the three-day time period, the nomination that is the subject of the advertising shall be withdrawn from eligibility for an Award.

With respect to any other advertising practices which, in the sole opinion of the Tony Awards Administration Committee, is deceptive to the public, the Tony Awards Administration Committee shall take whatever action is necessary to prevent such deceptive practices including, but not being limited to, withdrawal of a nominee's eligibility for an Award at any time prior to the announcement of the winner of the Award.

Eligible Theatres

Alvin Theatre
250 West 52 Street

Ambassador
215 West 49 Street

ANTA
245 West 52 Street

Brooks Atkinson
256 West 47 Street

Ethel Barrymore
243 West 47 Street

Martin Beck
302 West 45 Street

Belasco
111 West 44 Street

Bijou
209 West 45 Street

Biltmore
261 West 47 Street

Booth
222 West 45 Street

Broadhurst
235 West 44 Street

Broadway
1681 Broadway

Century
235 West 46 Street

Circle in the Square
1633 Broadway

Cort Theatre
138 West 48 Street

Edison
240 West 47 Street

46th Street
226 West 46 Street

Golden
252 West 45 Street

Helen Hayes
210 West 46 Street

Mark Hellinger
237 West 51 Street

Imperial	Palace
249 West 45 Street	1564 Broadway
Little	Playhouse
240 West 44 Street	357 West 48 Street
Longacre	Princess
220 West 48 Street	Broadway and 48 Street
Lunt-Fontanne	Plymouth
205 West 46 Street	236 West 45 Street
Lyceum	Rialto
149 West 45 Street	Broadway and 43 Street
Majestic	Billy Rose
245 West 44 Street	208 West 41 Street
Minskoff	Royale
200 West 45 Street	242 West 45 Street
Morosco	St. James
217 West 45 Street	246 West 44 Street
Music Box	Shubert
239 West 45 Street	225 West 44 Street
New Apollo	Uris
234 West 43 Street	1633 Broadway
Eugene O'Neill	Winter Garden
230 West 49 Street	1634 Broadway

Tony Winners *

A Chorus Line, 131,132, 133, 134
A Clearing in the Woods, 52
A Delicate Balance, 94
A Funny Thing Happened on the Way to the Forum, 76, 77, 78, 79, 114, 115
A Little Night Music, 119, 120, 121
A Majority of One, 57, 60
A Man for All Seasons, 71, 72, 73, 75
A Midsummer Night's Dream, 112
A Moon for the Misbegotten, 122, 124
A Shot in the Dark, 71
A Streetcar Named Desire, 26
A Taste of Honey, 68
A Thousand Clowns, 76
A Visit to a Small Planet, 52
Abbott, George, 43, 47, 65, 66, 79
Abrahams, Doris Cole, 127, 132
Abravanel, Maurice, 34
Adams, Edith, 50
Adams, Lee, 69, 109
Adler, Richard, 43, 44, 47
Adrian, Louis, 42
After the Fall, 81
Ain't Misbehavin', 140, 141
Albee, Edward, 78
Alberghetti, Anna Maria, 72
Albertson, Jack, 86
Alda, Robert, 35
Aldredge, Theoni V., 138
Alexander, Jane, 101
All My Sons, 25
All the Way Home, 68
Allen, Lewis, 136
Allen, Rae, 110
Allers, Franz, 52, 70
Alton, Robert, 38
And Miss Reardon Drinks A Little, 110
Anderson, Judith, 26
Angel in the Wings, 26
Anne of the Thousand Days, 27, 29
Annie, 135, 136, 137, 138
Another Part of the Forest, 25
Anouilh, Jean, 69
Antony and Cleopatra, 26
Antoon, A. J., 120
Any Wednesday, 81
Applause, 108, 109
Arkin, Alan, 76
Armistead, Horace, 27
Armstrong, Will Steven, 75

Aronson, Boris, 36, 96, 103, 113, 117, 133
Arthur, Beatrice, 91
As the Girls Go, 29
Ashley, Elizabeth, 72
Auberjonois, Rene, 108
Auntie Mame, 49, 52
Avian, Bob, 134, 146
Ayers, Lemuel, 28, 29
Azenberg, Emanuel, 141

Bacall, Lauren, 108
Baker, Lenny, 135
Baker Street, 89
Ballard, Lucinda, 25,75
Ballroom, 146
Balsam, Martin, 97
Bancroft, Anne, 54, 63
Barefoot in the Park, 83
Barr, Richard, 78, 145
Barrett, James Lee, 129
Bart, Lionel, 79
Bates, Alan, 118
Bay, Howard, 66, 93
Beaton, Cecil, 44, 52, 67, 109
Becket, 69, 70, 71
Bedford, Brian, 110
Bedroom Farce, 143
Begley, Ed, 45
Belafonte, Harry, 41
Bellamy, Ralph, 53
Bells Are Ringing, 50
Bennett, Michael, 116, 117, 125, 133, 134, 146
Berg, Gertrude, 57
Bergman, Ingrid, 25
Bernhardt, Melvin, 140
Bernstein, Aline, 34
Bernstein, Leonard, 39
Beverley, Trazana, 135
Big Fish, Little Fish, 68, 69
Bigley, Isabel, 35
Bishop, Carole, 131
Bissell, Richard, 43
Blackmer, Sidney, 33
Bless You All, 36
Bloomgarden, Kermit, 28, 39, 46, 56, 127
Blyden, Larry, 115
Bock, Jerry, 65, 66, 88, 89
Bolger, Ray, 28
Bolt, Robert, 72, 73
Bond, Sheila, 39

*Special Tony Award winners and all nominees listed throughout the book.

160